working

"That work is crucial not only to human subsistence but also to human flourishing is among the deepest insights of the Jewish and Christian traditions. At a time when work is more exploited than ever, Darby Ray presents thought-provoking alternatives, grounded in solidarity with everyday labor in which the divine is so deeply engaged."

Joerg Rieger, Ph.D.
Wendland-Cook Professor of Constructive Theology
Perkins School of Theology
Southern Methodist University

compass

Christian Explorations of Daily Living

David H. Jensen, Series Editor

Playing
James H. Evans Jr.

Shopping
Michelle A. Gonzalez

Working
Darby Kathleen Ray

Forthcoming Volumes

Eating and Drinking
Elizabeth Groppe

Parenting
David H. Jensen

Traveling
Joerg Rieger

Dreaming
Barbara Holmes

working

Darby Kathleen Ray

Fortress Press
Minneapolis

WORKING
Compass series
Christian Explorations of Daily Living

Cover design: Laurie Ingram
Book design: Christy J. P. Barker

Library of Congress Cataloging-in-Publication Data
Ray, Darby Kathleen
  Working / Darby Kathleen Ray.
    p. cm. — (Compass series : Christian explorations of daily living)
  Includes bibliographical references.
  ISBN 978-0-8006-9810-2 (alk. paper)
 1. Work—Religious aspects—Christianity. I. Title.
 BT738.5.R39 2011
 261.8'5—dc22
                    2011004840

Manufactured in the U.S.A.
15 14 13 12 11 1 2 3 4 5 6 7 8 9 10

contents

series foreword

Everyday practices matter for Christian faith. Our ordinary routines—eating, cooking, working, walking, shopping, playing, and parenting—are responses to the life God gives to the world. Christian faith claims that the ordinary materials and practices of human life are graced by God's presence: basic foodstuffs become the Body of Christ in a shared meal, water becomes the promise of new birth as ordinary people gather in Christ's name, and a transformed household becomes a metaphor for God's reign. Bodies, baths, meals, and households matter to Christian faith because God takes these everyday practices and materials as God's own: blessing, redeeming, and transforming them so that they more nearly reflect the hope and grace that come to us in the midst of the everyday. Christian faith does not flee from the everyday but embeds itself in daily, ordinary routines. This book series considers everyday practices as sites for theological reflection. When we pay close attention to everyday practices, we can glimpse classical Christian themes—redemption, creation, and incarnation—in new light. This book series does not attempt to *apply* classical doctrines to particular practices, but to offer narratives of ordinary routines, explore how immersion in them affects Christian life in a global world, and imagine how practice might re-form theology and theology re-form practice.

The series also explores the implications of globalization for daily practices and how these ordinary routines are implicated—for good and for ill—in the often-bewildering effects of an increasingly interconnected world. Everyday practices, after all, are the places where the global becomes local. We encounter globalization not in abstract theory, but in the routine affairs of shopping at the corner grocery for food grown on the other side of the globe, maintaining friendships with persons on other continents, fulfilling job responsibilities in workplaces where decisions ripple outward to seemingly distant neighbors. Daily practices put a human face on the complex phenomenon of globalization and offer one place to begin theological reflection on this phenomenon. Paying close attention to these practices helps unveil the injustice as well as the hope of a global world. Since unreflective and consumptive forms of these daily practices often manifest themselves in American consumer society, this series also offers concrete suggestions for how daily practices might be reconfigured to more nearly reflect the hope and justice given to the world by God's grace. If daily practices implicate our complicity in global injustice, they might also be sites to imagine that world alternatively.

Though each book displays an organization uniquely its own, every title in the series offers three common themes: (1) The books offer thick descriptions of particular practices in North American society. What do parenting, cooking, and dressing look like in American communities in the twenty-first century? (2) The books survey varied Christian understandings of each practice, summoning theological resources for enhanced understanding and critique of typical forms of practice. What have Christians said about eating, dreaming, and traveling throughout their history, and how do their reflections matter today? (3) The books offer a constructive restatement of each practice and explore how ordinary practices might reshape or sharpen beliefs and themes of Christian faith. How does attention to practice affect the way we understand Christian theology, and how does attention to theology affect the way we understand everyday practice? Each book shares the conviction that Christian life is best encountered (and often best understood) in the midst of the ordinary.

Many authors of these volumes are members of the Workgroup in Constructive Theology, an ecumenical group of teachers and scholars who write and teach theology in dialogue with contemporary critiques of Christian traditions. We are diverse in theological and denominational orientation yet share the recognition that Christian theology has often been employed for abusive ends. Theological traditions have silenced women, people of color, the poor, and gay/lesbian/bisexual/transgender (GLBT) persons. Our constructive restatements of Christian practice, therefore, do not simply restate classical Christian traditions, but question them as we learn from them. We listen to the past while we also critique it, just as we hope subsequent generations will also criticize and learn from us. Because so many voices have been silenced throughout the church's history, it is essential that Christian theologians attend to voices beyond the corridors of ecclesial and social power. Outside these corridors, after all, is where Christian faith takes root in ordinary life. Though each of us writes theology somewhat differently— some with explicit schools of theology in mind, such as liberationist or womanist theology—we all share the conviction that theology *matters*, not simply for reflective life, but for the life of the world. Christian theology, at its best, is one expression of life's fullness and flourishing. Our words, in other words, ought to point to a more abundant life of grace in the face of the death-dealing forces at work on an economically stratified and ecologically threatened planet.

We have written each book with a minimum of technical jargon, intending them to be read in a wide variety of settings. The books may be used in seminary and undergraduate courses, including introductions to theology, ethics, and

Christian spirituality. Clergy will also find them useful as they seek brief yet substantive books on Christian life that will inform their work of preaching, counseling, and teaching. We also imagine that each text could be used in churches for adult education classes. Many Christians seek guides for how faith is lived but are disenchanted with conservative approaches that shun dialogue with the wider culture of religious diversity. This series offers a progressive, culturally engaged approach to daily practices, globalization, and Christian theology. We think the books are as important in the questions they ask as in the answers they attempt.

David H. Jensen, series editor

preface

We human beings spend a lot of time working. Whether we log hours in an office, store, factory, or field for a regular paycheck; whether we cook, clean, and care for children as we make a home for ourselves and others; whether we write, paint, or play music in the hopes that the fruits of these labors might one day be appreciated by others, we spend many hours of each day engaged in work. Work has been around as long as our species has walked the earth. As long as humans have worked, we have spent time complaining, celebrating, lamenting, and rejoicing in work. Most of us work in order to live: work helps secure enough food for us to survive and provide a roof over our heads. But many work and do not partake in these basics of a humane life. Hard work, in a world of vast economic disparity, does not necessarily result in a living wage. In our day, as in the past, work can become unforgiving and backbreaking, a drudgery that is little more than slavery. Others struggle to find work, a reality that has become increasingly visible during this time of global economic recession. Yet, as many seek work, others become addicted to work in the hopes of securing more consumer goods.

Darby Ray's study of work attends to each of these realities and the distortions of work that have become prevalent in our day. She acknowledges the pain of work as well as its promise. Though work can degrade persons and destroy the environment, its real purpose, in light of the Christian story, is to form persons and construct the world. This timely and thoughtful book offers an unvarnished glimpse at some of the problems facing work and workers in our day, mines the Christian scriptures and the history of its reflection on work for fresh wisdom to address those problems, and offers a sacramental vision for work that focuses on subsistence, selfhood, and service. The result is a renewed call for workers to partake in the abundance of life and to work so that all might take part in an economy characterized by grace and gift, rather than exchange and competition. And for that to take place, there still is a lot of work to do.

David H. Jensen

introduction

It is Labor Day, and I am sandwiched in the backseat between my two school-aged daughters. Driving from Stanton, Nebraska, to Independence, Missouri, we three are southerners on a Midwest sojourn. Commenting on the now-familiar agricultural expanse, my eleven-year-old sarcastically exclaims, "Look, Mom, *more* corn!" I begin to opine about how farming and food production have been transformed in the past few decades—the "from family farm to global agribusiness" narrative—but the kids aren't interested, and my Missouri relatives in the front seat have had enough of that sad tale. Hours in the car offer ample time for reflection. On this national "day of rest," I am pondering work.

Like millions of other Americans on this particular Labor Day, I feel profoundly blessed simply to have a job. During this Great Recession, unemployment has reached a twenty-five-year high. Millions of people have given up looking for work and thus aren't even included in that statistic, and millions more have had their hours cut or are settling for part-time work. The talk around the kitchen table last week was of three more family friends who had lost their jobs. These days, it seems like everybody knows somebody who is unemployed. People are still firing up the grills and slicing the watermelon this Labor Day, but there is caution in the air. Suddenly, that statistic about most Americans being only a paycheck away from poverty is too close for comfort.

Some of us have lost our homes, moving back in with Mom and Dad at record-setting rates, slogging from one friend or coworker's sofa to another, or joining the growing ranks of those sleeping in cars, vans, and trucks. Others of us have lost jobs or found our hours and/or benefits reduced. Debt-financing shenanigans may have been a major cause of this recession, and sociologist Zygmunt Bauman may be right that most of us suffer from "debt addiction," but credit cards are the only thing keeping increasing numbers of us afloat these days.[1] Never mind the mounting finance charges and impossible balances; we depend on credit cards to buy groceries and pay the car note. Fingers crossed we won't need medical care.

Even those of us with good, secure jobs are feeling the squeeze in the form of salary and hiring freezes, budget reductions, and rising health insurance premiums, not to mention the pressure to work harder, faster, and longer as employers try to increase productivity with a reduced workforce and decreased spending. At times like this, people with jobs tend to hunker down. With the casualties of economic downturn all around, many work longer hours without asking for overtime pay, while others choose not to act on grievances against employers; collective action on behalf of workers can seem an irrational distraction. Such responses can function as a shot in the arm to the economy, resulting in higher productivity and, eventually, increased profit for owners, managers, and stockholders, but they also threaten to undermine worker well-being in the long run.

Surely, better days are ahead. We respond to the occasional whisper of "economic recovery" or "modest job growth" with dreams of fatter, less-anxious times. Even so, what millions of middle-class Americans are experiencing during this global recession—the instability, the pressure, the material loss and emotional trauma—is merely a taste of what our lower-wage compatriots live with day in and day out, with little or no hope of "recovery." For them, these particular hard times may be getting a lot of media attention but are not especially new.

When we consider the gamut of work and workers today, it is easy to see that work isn't working particularly well, at least not for millions and millions of honest, industrious Americans whose labor is rewarded with far less than the well-being it should nurture. Whether we're overworked, underworked, or out of work, we Christians probably ought to be getting a little worked up about work. This short book is a kind of guide to that process. It begins with a portrait of work and workers in today's complex, globalized world (chapter 1), considers insights into work from Christian scriptures (chapter 2) and tradition (chapter 3), and offers reflections and proposals for how Christians today might interpret and navigate with integrity, compassion, and imagination the turbulent worlds of work in which we find ourselves (chapter 4). The ideas developed in the book build on the thoughtful labors of a multitude of scholars and practitioners, only a fraction of whose names appear in its pages. More than anything, this book has been shaped by the hundreds of Millsaps College students who have taken my course, "The Meaning of Work," over the years.

Each fall, about twenty-five young people and I embark on a fourteen-week journey together, pondering formative texts, movements, and ideas about work. In addition to reading important works written by famous thinkers from the past, we consider contemporary descriptions and analyses from diverse sources, including the "texts" of students' own lives—their family's work history, for example, and their own diverse forays into working. We also engage in a hands-on cost-of-living experiment in which students attempt to make ends meet on a low-wage worker's income. After interviewing real low-wage workers, students gather in small groups to search for decent housing, shop for groceries, decipher a city bus schedule, develop a monthly budget, and consider how they would pay for things like clothing and medical care.

What if they had to include a child in the calculus? Back to the drawing board they go, visiting the public school near the apartment they thought they could afford and thinking about after-school and enrichment options for "their" child. Or how about retirement? What would that look like when the only relevant "benefit" their low-wage job offers is an employee savings plan without a dollar of employer contribution? This assignment tends to function as a reality check for my bright and ambitious young students, opening their eyes to how much it costs simply to subsist in today's world and how difficult it is to attain life's most basic necessities on a low-wage income. It also sends them back to those famous philosophers, theologians, and political theorists with a new cadre of questions and challenges.

As a result of that course, I find myself each fall immersed in thoughts about working—considerations of work's function and meaning, questions about its organization and its economic and social valuation, and worries about the impact of these things on the everyday lives of workers. Most of my students will eventually join the professional and managerial classes, so the opportunity to walk a mile in a low-wage worker's shoes could be transformative. In addition, the practice of stepping back from work to ask about its motivations, aims, and outcomes, and especially about its relationship to the public good, may also inform my students' future work practices, and perhaps also those of the readers of this book. The role of religion in shaping attitudes toward work is also an important dimension of the course we engage in together and is usually an entirely new set of considerations for my students.

This book on working is, then, an outgrowth of a decade's journey with young people in Jackson, Mississippi. We engage the topic of work from the context of a small liberal arts college in the middle of the poorest state in the nation. Our lovely campus is only a few blocks from the state capitol, from impressive medical centers, museums, business complexes, restaurants, concert halls, and genteel neighborhoods. It is also barely a stone's throw from chronic unemployment and underemployment and the intergenerational poverty and problems they breed. My students have a world of opportunity at their fingertips and a world of suffering at their backs. In this context, they have been brave and thoughtful interlocutors on the complex subject of working, and I have been privileged to share the conversation with them. This small book is in debt to numerous others as well, including faculty and staff colleagues at Millsaps College; friends and partners in the Midtown and Mid-City neighborhoods of Jackson; Don Compier and his generous Community of Christ colleagues in Independence, Missouri; members of the Workgroup in Constructive Theology, especially Dave Jensen; and Michael West and his wonderful colleagues at Fortress Press. My family, especially Sharon, Pamela, Raymond, Chandler, and Elena, provided vital hospitality, patience, and good humor. For their work in support of my work, I am deeply grateful.

1

working: beyond survival

Would you work if you didn't have to? Seriously. If you didn't need the money, would you still work?

We may moan and groan about work—the hours, the boss, the pay, the pace—but the vast majority of us cannot imagine life without it. In fact, we insist we would work even if we didn't need to. What is it about work that is so compelling?

At the most basic level, we work to survive. But if there were ever a time when that was work's only function, it has long since passed. Sure, we labor so that we can have food, shelter, and clothing, but in today's world, even the poorest among us hopes for more from work than mere necessities. As Immanuel Kant knew in the eighteenth century, work gives our lives content—not merely a way of *getting* things, but something to *do*. Paid or unpaid, work endows our daily lives with structure, routine, and purpose. Through work, we act on the world around us. We attempt to hammer out a place for ourselves and those for whom we feel responsible. Even in its most modest incarnations, work is

> Paid or unpaid, work endows our daily lives with structure, routine, and purpose.

a world-structuring, meaning-making enterprise. Without it, the world portends chaos and threatens meaning.

Jamaal is a fifth-grader who lives a stone's throw from my office. We meet twice a week to work on his reading. He shares a small rental house with his mother, an aunt, two young cousins, and two siblings in their twenties. No one in Jamaal's family has steady work. In fact, only one person on his whole street has a regular, forty-hour-a-week job in the formal economy.

One of the most devastating developments of recent years in the United States is the emergence of what sociologist William Julius Wilson identifies as jobless neighborhoods: "poor, segregated neighborhoods in which a majority of adults are either unemployed or have dropped out of the labor force altogether."[1] America's inner cities are rife with these "jobless ghettos," and in them, the absence of work's world-structuring dynamic is dramatically felt. Without the routine, stability, and discipline that work imposes, "life, including family life, becomes less coherent." When one lives not only in poverty but in a world where work has all but disappeared, then one is missing a lot more than money and its products. Says Wilson: "In the absence of regular employment, a person lacks not only a place in which to work and the receipt of regular income but also a coherent organization of the present—that is, a system of concrete expectations and goals."[2] Imagine the consequences for children who grow up without such a framework of meaning and behavior, without an adult population to model and encourage the skills and habits likely to produce positive social outcomes. Without the structure and purpose cultivated by work, the world would seem a strange and unwelcoming place.

No matter where our work falls on spectra of income or social status, and regardless of any other reasons (conscious or subconscious) we might have, the vast majority of us work to attain life's basic material necessities *and* to live in a world that is coherent and has meaning. To survive in a world that makes sense is something we all desire and, moreover, something we *need*. It was no doubt in recognition of the foundational material and existential role of work in human life that the General Assembly of the United Nations included in its 1948 Universal Declaration of Human Rights the right to work: "Everyone has the right to work, to free choice of employment, to just and favourable conditions of work and to protection against unemployment."[3] A universal right—work is *that* fundamental to human existence.

> "Everyone has the right to work, to free choice of employment, to just and favourable conditions of work and to protection against unemployment."

I'm at a Christmas party at a friend's house, hoping no one notices that I'm camped out by the spinach dip. An unfamiliar person approaches, fixes a plate, and nods. I nod back, swallowing quickly.

"Hello, I'm Darby," I say.

"Lauren Nichols. Nice to meet you. How's the spinach dip?"

"Quite good, actually."

"So, Darby, what do you do?"

Most of us are familiar with this new-acquaintance, "What do you do?" mantra, by which the inquirer means only one thing: What is your work? Knowing one's work, it is assumed, sheds important light on one's real identity. Beyond survival and an often-inchoate psychological-conceptual framework for living, we work because it establishes and sustains our individual identity or sense of self. Perhaps most dramatically in the United States but also elsewhere in the world, personal identity and social esteem are powerfully grounded in work. This fact helps explain the anxiety felt by so many people as they approach retirement. The prospect of rest is usually welcome, but one fears it will be accompanied by a loss of self. Without our work, who are we? Without our identity as workers, where in the world do we fit?

We might expect that such questions and concerns are the special province of the privileged. After all, it is easy to imagine why people with high-status jobs would identify themselves with their work. However, one need look no further than the garbage cans of cities like San Francisco to see that the work-identity connection is vibrant across social and economic divides.

Meet the underground recyclers—homeless men and women who forage through other people's trash in search of recyclable items, then haul those items to recycling centers for remuneration.[4] From one perspective, this is desperate, dirty, dehumanizing labor, but from another, it is surprisingly principled work that endows its practitioners with dignity and self-respect against all odds. This work is not for the faint of heart. It involves long hours in the elements, often at night, and requires physical strength, street smarts, and business acumen. A lucky few have vans or cars for storing and transporting recyclables, but most use shopping carts, which they push for miles as they work their routes, digging through unsorted trash in search of neglected recyclables. Homeless recyclers like Dobie, an African American man who works a prosperous San Francisco neighborhood, have clear work territories and build long-standing partnerships with business owners and apartment managers. As sociologist Teresa Gowan tells us, "These relationships are often referred to in formal business language: 'I try not to default on my schedule,' says Dobie. 'I've got several long-standing accounts in the Castro area,' says Jordan," a former forklift operator who was laid off.[5]

Dobie, Jordan, and others find themselves ousted by the formal economy, pushed out of jobs and homes and onto the streets, but their sense of self is so powerfully connected to work that they find "jobs" in the informal economy, and they work those jobs with discipline and commitment. While the wider society associates homelessness with sloth and other forms of moral deviance, Gowan's study reveals that homeless recyclers typically embrace normative moral standards and have a robust work ethic. Where others think of them as subhuman social parasites, these men and women define themselves as *selves* by asserting themselves as workers. Gowan's account of Sam, a middle-aged white man who eventually died next to his recycling cart, illustrates the self-work relationship:

> The first time I ever met him he told me a story of an argument with a "resident" the night before. "Hey, keep the noise down, I've got to *work* in the morning," the man had shouted out of a window. "What do you think I'm doing," Sam shouted in return. "They just don't think, you know," he said in retrospect. "They think we do this for fun or something. I work hard, I clear up the neighborhood. Don't beg, don't steal, don't deal drugs. You'd think people could be civil to me."[6]

For Sam and other homeless people who occupy "an extraordinarily dehumanizing and frightening location on the American social map," hard work enables self-definition and self-respect. Underscoring the self-defining, dignity-producing power of work, Gowan concludes: "Given their stigmatized social position, recyclers are choosing to concentrate their efforts on using their work to redefine themselves as people with full humanity rather than victims [or monsters]. In this way they not only pull themselves back into the flows of capital, but also create self-respect in a hostile world."[7]

So we work because it provides us with the basics we need to survive. Work gives our lives content and coherence. Work is a primary avenue toward self-definition and self-respect. What else does work give us? Why else do we work? We noticed in our discussion of homeless recyclers that work has social value. It positions us in relation to others in the world. For Sam, being fully human meant being a worker, even though his particular work put him near the bottom of the social hierarchy. Still, the homeless recyclers Gowan studied proudly place themselves above "stiffs" and "winos"—the unemployed homeless—and in so doing, they reinforce the social stratification system imposed by work in today's world. Thus, we see that another basic function of work is to demarcate social roles and, by extension, distribute social power. For those at the bottom of the hierarchy, as for those at the top, we work in part to get onto the social map, to have a place in relation to others. Despite the obvious inequalities of that map, we learn from Sam and his homeless recycling peers that any place is better than no place at all. In today's world, work more than anything else is what bestows social place.

Making a Mark
"I clear up the neighborhood."

Work is not only a prime means by which we are positioned within and encoded by society. It is also an important means for shaping society, for making our own imprint. Through work, we are actors in and on the world. We make a difference. We leave our mark. While work's transformative potential is probably most easily accessed by those with work that includes relatively more autonomy and social value, we should not forget that Sam's self-respect is rooted partly in the belief that his work has genuine social value: "I clear up the neighborhood." Low-wage workers such as garment industry employees in Boston's Chinatown reiterate the importance of making a positive contribution to the larger society with one's work. As one seamstress notes, "There are three things that each person needs—food, house, clothing—and we take care of one of these. The clothes we do are everywhere, keeping the children, the grown men and women, warm and well."[8] Even within the constraints of low-wage employment, work is a primary means of shaping the world we live in.

Of course, even as we can appreciate that work is a vital means for making an impact on the world, we should not ignore that some of us have far more opportunity for constructive engagement with the world through our work than do others. We would like to think that the days of oppressive work routines and conditions are long gone, but they are rampant in today's postindustrial economy and, by some measures, are even on the rise. Thus, while work can be a means for shaping the world we live in and, ideally, making a positive difference, such individual agency assumes a degree of freedom and creativity that many jobs exclude.

Related to this notion of work as a way of shaping the world is the relatively recent idea that work should be a form of self-expression, a means or outlet for personal growth. Increasingly, we assume work should be personally fulfilling. Work should present us with meaningful opportunities to express ourselves and actualize our gifts. Advertising taglines like "It's not just our job, it's our passion" promote everything from health care to beer brewing. A favorite piece of career advice offered to young people is "Find something you love to do, and then figure out how to get paid for it." The message here is that work is where we explore or activate our passions. Work is where we do what we love, where we are engaged and fulfilled. Work is a means of self-realization, even a "calling." My mother tells the story of the scruffy young man she and my father hired to do some work on their house. One day the young man called my mother outside and directed her gaze at a small area of cement at the bottom of an exterior wall of the house. When it was clear my mother didn't know what she was looking at, he said, "Don't you see the swirls—the movement and rhythm of the stucco? I'm a stucco *artist*."

No matter what kind of work we do, some of us have work that is genuinely self-actualizing. Others do their best to squeeze drops of meaning and affirmation out of mostly miserable jobs. When we pause to consider this latter group, we might wonder whether the work-as-personal-fulfillment notion that has become a kind of cultural ideal in our time is such a good idea. In a society already powerfully stratified by work roles, pay scales, and benefits packages (or lack thereof), the romanticizing of work via the idea of work as self-actualization may create one more stratifying dynamic. As philosopher Lars Svendsen notes, "The amount of intrinsic satisfaction is clearly not equally distributed among jobs."[9] The idea that work should be a means to personal growth and fulfillment may actually compound the misery of those whose work does not measure up—that is, the vast majority of workers in the world today.

The Handmaiden of Consumerism

> *consumption (noun)—a progressive wasting away of the body; tuberculosis; the utilization of economic goods in the satisfaction of wants or in the process of production resulting chiefly in their destruction, deterioration, or transformation.*[10]

Thus far, we have recognized work as a means of physical survival, existential coherence, self-respect, social integration, individual agency, and self-actualization. We conclude this brief overview of work's role in contemporary living by acknowledging that, increasingly, its main function is to enable consumption. Arguably, work's most dominant role these days is to keep the wheels of consumer culture turning. Put simply, we work so that we can buy. Of course, we have always worked in order to procure what we need to live, and since the institution of wage labor, we have worked for money and then spent that money on the things we need. The difference today is that we spend our money at unprecedented rates and on things we don't need. In truth, however, the point is not to buy in order to fulfill a need, but simply to buy. It doesn't even matter if we actually consume or use what we buy; the constant acquisition is the thing. Sam and his recycling peers may be products of an advanced capitalist economy, but they are "old world" in grounding their identity in work. Increasingly, we articulate our humanity less by working than by buying. It is how we participate in today's world. Rich or poor, buying is how we integrate into society, how we express our membership in the human race. "I shop, therefore I am."

> Arguably, work's most dominant role these days is to keep the wheels of consumer culture turning.

Work is still important, but less for its intrinsic value than for its instrumental value. In the new economy, work's big claim to fame is that it is the precondition of consumption. Work earns the money with which we acquire new goods. From this standpoint, the inequalities in working conditions and in the social valuation of different kinds of work are no longer as important as they were even a generation ago because the main thing that matters about work is that it yields money for buying things. Thanks to discount stores, cheap labor, credit cards, and ever-advancing production technologies, there is a cornucopia of products even low-wage workers can aim to acquire. Thus, low-wage workers can deflect the negative stigma that once accompanied their devalued jobs by being "good" consumers—that is, by keeping up with the latest consumer trends and fashions, even if in cheap imitation. These days, social shame is caused less by a "low-class" job than by the inability to keep up with the normative buying pace. The pressure to keep up as consumers is intense. For my family, the damaging effects hit home with particular force last summer when a childhood friend of my sister was shot dead, along with her two children, by a husband and father who by all accounts was loving, devoted, and hardworking, but who simply could not cope with a downsizing family economy and the impossibility of maintaining the consumer lifestyle to which he and his family had become accustomed. Rather than face the social shame of a downsized existence, he took his own life and his family's. Without adequate buying power, life was apparently not worth living.

While work's primary function today is often to enable acquisition, work is the precondition of consumption in another way, as well. Increasingly, work involves the production and sale of a fast-changing array of consumer goods and services. In other words, more and more of us have work whose very content contributes to a buying-centered way of being. Our work produces something that is intentionally short-term, designed to last only a brief time and then be replaced by a newer model. Whether we are the low-wage pieceworker in the clothing industry, the barely middle-class clerk who sells that clothing in a local department or discount store, the upper-middle-class corporate buyer or advertiser of that line of clothing, or the millionaire designer who developed the fashion trend that inspired the clothing, our work's real contribution to the world is to stoke the fires of consumption.

Work's Deformation

When I ask Jamaal how many books he has at home, he just shakes his head and looks away. A moment later, he glances up with animated eyes: "But I got a new game for my DS last week!"

This most recent incarnation of work—as the handmaiden of contemporary consumer culture—has consequences for the other functions of work previously discussed. Indeed, it deforms each one of them in worrisome ways. Here, we can gesture only briefly toward these deformations, beginning with the most obvious: If our work is funding an indefatigable consumer appetite, then our ability to secure life's basic necessities (work as survival) is reduced. Especially for those near the bottom of the work/wage hierarchy, this refocusing of work's remuneration from genuine needs to market-induced desires leaves individuals, families, and communities starved of the resources necessary for dignified subsistence living. And so we see tragedies like children who have the latest electronic gadgets or the year's trendiest sneakers but no books at home or food in the refrigerator. A similar kind of deconstruction happens as consumerism's exaltation of instant gratification and short-term commitments undermines the kind of discipline, regularity, and long-term perspective inculcated by regular employment. Here, the coherent framework for purposeful living that in previous generations was cultivated by work comes unraveled under the impress of consumerism's frenetic pace and short-term horizon.

We don't all need to feel as if our work is saving the world, but we do yearn to contribute something real, something worthwhile with our labor.

When it comes to work as a means of self-respect, we find that here, too, today's consumer culture can deaden work's character-building potential. We don't all need to feel as if our work is saving the world, but we do yearn to contribute something real, something worthwhile with our labor. The fact that so much of today's work is connected to products designed to last only a short time, and services that respond to or fuel spurious consumption, means the link between work and self-respect is tenuous. As for the cultivation of social integration and responsibility, we see that what puts one on the social map within contemporary consumer culture is increasingly not work but acquisition. We also learn that one of the key expressions of social responsibility, especially during times of national crisis, is shopping. Love your country? Why, then get to the mall or go to Disney World! Oh, yes, and work hard so you can buy what you want when you're there.

Work's historic role as provider of meaningful opportunities to engage and shape one's world is also eroding rapidly under the weight of consumer culture. If shopping has become an important civic duty, it is because "the world" has been redefined to mean Walmart and Wall Street. Leaving our mark on *that* world is less a matter of working hard than of spending steadily, of investing our money, time, and creative energy in the consumer market. Once again, work's main value is its bankrolling of that investment.

By now, it should be easy to appreciate the ways in which the trend toward work as self-actualization can feed right into consumerism's priorities. Indeed, it is such an easy fit that one wonders whether perhaps this whole notion of work isn't itself a product of corporate America. After all, when one's work is one's "passion" or personal "calling," then one happily devotes ever more time and personal resources to it. It can hardly be coincidence that the class of workers most likely to speak of work in terms of passion, self-expression, and self-actualization—that is, today's "knowledge workers"—are the same ones who log the longest hours on the job and identify themselves the most closely with their work. They are also, not incidentally, the ones who spend the most time away from home and family. Work as self-actualization, indeed.

Looking Back on Work

We live today in what scholars call "the new economy." Although there is strong consensus about what constitutes this new economy—its defining features and driving forces—there is lively debate about just how "new" it really is. The shape and organization of work, as well as the consequences for workers, are at the heart of the debate.

Now one of the very first requirements for a man who is fit to handle pig iron as a regular occupation is that he shall be so stupid and so phlegmatic that he more nearly resembles in his mental make-up the ox than any other type.

Frederick Taylor
The Principles of Scientific Management, 1911

To appreciate what is new about today's world of work, it helps to understand the "old" against which the new defines itself. When scholars speak of old modes of work, they typically invoke Henry Ford and the modern industrial work methods embraced by the Ford Motor Company (tagged "Fordism"). At the heart of these techniques was the division of labor—the divvying up of complex work tasks to increase efficiency and productivity. For classic proponents of this "modern" technique, the goal of ever-greater efficiency and productivity meant the end of the traditional craft-based, apprentice system of work in which a master craftsman was the master of both conceptual work knowledge and physical technique. This craftsman passed the skill and artistry of the craft to younger generations through sustained mentoring relationships. Such an arrangement was deemed a waste of time and money by people like Charles Babbage and Frederick Taylor, who argued that complex work tasks should be converted into a series of simplified tasks performed by unskilled workers. Instead of paying highly skilled workers to perform a range of tasks, companies began to assign low-skilled (and low-paid) workers to perform only low-skill tasks, as in Taylor's description of the worker who handles pig iron:

> Now one of the very first requirements for a man who is fit to handle pig iron as a regular occupation is that he shall be so stupid and so phlegmatic that he more nearly resembles in his mental make-up the ox than any other type. The man who is mentally alert and intelligent is for this very reason entirely unsuited for what would, for him, be the grinding monotony of work of this character. Therefore the workman who is best suited to handling pig iron is unable to understand the real science of doing this class of work. He is so stupid that the word "percentage" has no meaning to him, and he must consequently be trained by a man more intelligent than himself into the habit of working in accordance with the laws of this science before he can be successful.[11]

Moreover, insisted the prophets of modern industrial technique, the knowledge of work should not be held captive by the workers themselves but should become the province of a new class of managers. Out with the master craftsman, in with the manager. The thinking was that when complex work tasks are divided by management into simple, discrete steps that require little thought or skill, and when each step is completed with the greatest economy of movement, then efficiency will improve, production increase, payrolls decrease, and profits grow. The goal of standardization reaches its logical conclusion in mechanization, where the variability of human labor is replaced with the predictability of the machine whenever possible.

Henry Ford's institution of these work innovations led, as predicted, to astonishing improvements in efficiency and productivity. Given the shortage of skilled labor with which Ford was confronted in his day, the standardization and mechanization of work seemed the perfect solution. Workers on his assembly lines did not need to master a craft; they just needed to follow directions and work hard and fast. Ironically, Ford imposed a work style that reduced worker autonomy and individuality even as he (and they) developed a product that has contributed more than any other to the world's staunchest individualism. The mass production of the automobile had the effect of siphoning American political and economic will away from mass transit, fueling a national ethos in which the individual trumps the collective at almost every turn.

Like wildfire, the techniques and logic of mass production spread around the globe and to every industry. The upside was the broad availability and affordability of uniformly produced goods of all sorts—the promise of "a material cornucopia for all," as sociologist Stephen Meyer puts it.[12] The downside was the deskilling of the workforce, the loss of the versatility and workmanship of the craft ideal, and the growing power, pay, and prestige differential between workers and managers/owners.

In his own treatment of workers, Henry Ford was atypically humane—a fact that incited the ire of his peers. Ford paid his workers what we today would recognize as a living wage—a wage that allows one to live a modest but dignified life—and he instituted a more humane (forty-hour) workweek. A businessman through and through, Ford was motivated not so much by humanitarian impulse as by the conviction that it would improve worker retention and productivity and, equally important, enable his workers to become good consumers who would buy the very products their work helped create. Ford, however, was the clear exception here. Most owners of production used the fact of a largely low-skilled, disempowered workforce to keep wages as low as possible, workweeks as long as possible, and concerns about workplace safety and environmental impact as marginal as possible. Thus, as Meyer notes, "the new industrial technology" that scholars refer to as Fordism "was a mixed social blessing, perhaps even a curse." It yielded impressive gains in production, consumption, and profit, but it also contained "incredible social costs."[13]

Work in the "New" Economy

Today's "new economy" is arguably a very different world. Gone are the days when a young man followed his father into "company work" and remained there for life, gradually working his way up the pay and prestige scale until retiring at age sixty-five with a modest but livable pension. Gone are the days when manufacturing work was dominated by Fordist regimes of organization, technique, and power. Only a minority of us actually make anything tangible with our work. Instead, the vast majority of us deliver intangible goods or services. Not only is the content of most work different these days, but its organization also has changed dramatically, as has the skill set required to do it and even the "temporality" of work.[14] Still, vestiges of the past remain, for better and worse. In the rest of this chapter, we consider several of the defining features of work in the new economy by engaging specific worlds of work.

We begin with the manufacturing world, where the changes in the past thirty years have been so profound that they have generated a new scholarly school of thought known as post-Fordism. Those who characterize today's world of work as post-Fordist argue that, thanks to microprocessor technologies and changes in consumer markets, work has shifted away from the rigid, standardized, and often dehumanizing methods and relationships of the past and toward a more flexible, open-ended, and humane set of practices.[15] According to this school of thought, the world of mass production has undergone a profound transformation. Instead of massive factories that stay in the same location for generations and employ a stable workforce, information technologies and fast-paced consumer demand have made small-batch, flexible production a reality. And where the machine designs of yesteryear lent themselves to a deskilled workforce and rigid worker-management polarizations, today's computer-based machinery requires a reskilled workforce, a return to a certain level of "craft" sensibility and discretion, and the softening of the formerly sharp division between workers and management. In this "kinder, gentler" post-Fordist world of production, workers are purportedly empowered to bring not only their manual skills to work but also their "intellective" skills—to integrate body and mind in pursuit of a holistic and productive work experience. Work in this paradigm, say post-Fordists, is no longer directed primarily by bureaucratic control but by organizational commitment.

With computerization I am further away from my job than I have ever been before.

Too good to be true? When sociologists of work conduct reality checks on these post-Fordist predictions about work, many of them conclude that while massive transformations in manufacturing technique and culture have indeed occurred, many of the negative features of Fordism nevertheless stubbornly persist. The pulp and paper industry is a case in point. Shoshana Zuboff's study of two mills making the transition during the 1980s to a computer-centered manufacturing environment reveals that for workers, and perhaps in the long run for industry owners as well, the shift entailed profound losses. Most dramatic for workers was the disappearance of work's rich sentience. Where once they had monitored the pulp's progress through sight, smell, touch, and even taste, now they do so by watching a computer monitor from a separate space. As they shifted from physical proximity and embodied engagement to virtual surveillance and data interfaces, workers experienced a new kind of alienation—the loss of tangible connection to one's work, as expressed compellingly by a mill worker:

> With computerization I am further away from my job than I have ever been before. I used to listen to the sounds the boiler makes and know just how it was running. I could look at the fire in the furnace and tell by its color how it was burning. I knew what kinds of adjustments were needed by the shades of color I saw. . . . Now I only have numbers to go by.[16]

According to post-Fordist theory, this loss is actually a sign of progress because workers are developing new, higher-order skills that make them more competent to live and work in contemporary society. It is argued that the move from embodied to abstract knowledge enhances the value of workers and reduces the skill/knowledge difference between workers and managers—in effect, flattening out hierarchies of power and prestige that once kept workers subjugated.

In contrast to the theory, however, Steven Vallas and John Beck found that in the manufacturing sector they studied, the old hierarchical logic was still solidly in place, albeit with a new look. At the top of the manufacturing power ladder these days are white-collar workers with computer science or engineering degrees who often view the embodied knowledge of the majority of shop floor workers as backward, prescientific, and unreliable when compared with their own computer-based knowledge. As one process engineer admits,

It drives me *crazy* when operators say you can't control the whole process with the computers. They'll stand there and scrape the stock with their thumbnail, and say they can tell me more about the stock than the $40 million Accuray nuclear instruments we just installed! They're just feeling threatened by us, like all their secrets are being taken away, and they don't like that at all.[17]

Instead of *enhancing* worker discretion and autonomy per the post-Fordist model, those in authority at the mills Vallas and Beck studied worry that workers have too much freedom—that their way of knowing poses a threat to the legitimacy of scientific knowledge and to the company's bottom line, and hence needs to be curtailed by more standardized work regimes. Ironically, engineers tend to assume that if and when computerized systems crash or malfunction, manual know-how will fill the gap until things are back on line; however, the devaluation of the old embodied knowledge is leading to its rapid obsolescence, so the industry may face a permanent loss with unforeseen consequences. Those in the post-Fordist school of thought declare that contemporary transformations of work are good for workers, enhancing their skill base and autonomy and reducing workplace power inequities. However, evidence from the manufacturing sector paints a less sanguine picture. This evidence suggests that as "knowledge work" increases in economic and social value, "body work" and its local, experiential knowledge undergo a corresponding devaluation, creating an ever-expanding chasm between kinds of work and workers.

When we create this kind of bifurcated picture of work, says author Mike Rose, we show our class bias and blindness. Our trumpeting of the complexity and rigor of knowledge work at the expense of other kinds of work reflects our own myopia, our inability to see the intelligence at work in manual labor and blue-collar work: "The mental processes that enable service. The aesthetics of physical labor. The complex interplay of the social and the mechanical. The choreography of hand, eye, ear, brain. The everpresence of abstraction, planning, and problem solving in everyday work."[18] Rose offers a thick description of several kinds of blue-collar work, from waitressing to long-haul truck driving, to demonstrate that in spite of the new economy's narrow definition and robust affirmation of knowledge work, the mind is impressively at work in "lower-class" forms of work as well.

In addition to the shift toward knowledge work, other hallmarks of the new economy are globalization, flexibility, and mobility. We can look to the apparel industry for insight into how these features of contemporary capitalism are reshaping the world of work.

Even if celebrity magazines and hit TV shows aren't our thing, we are aware of how quickly fashion trends change in today's world. Especially in women's apparel, but also increasingly in children's and kids' and men's areas, the pace of change is mind-boggling. To keep up with the market's insistence on constant consumption, an endless stream of novel trends and products must be brought to market (and advertised, to create demand for them). More than perhaps any other sector of the economy, the apparel industry must be fast-moving and flexible. In this respect, it is on the cutting edge of the new global economy. Apparel is also the most globalized of industries, with fads going cross-continental in a matter of days and production moving around the globe almost as fast.

It is interesting to note that despite being on the economic cutting edge, the apparel industry's basic method of production is not at all new. A woman bent over a sewing machine—that's how my mother sewed my clothes when I was a child, and that's how it is still done today. "In some ways," note sociologists Edna Bonacich and Richard Appelbaum, "the apparel industry is the epitome of free market capitalism because the barriers to entry are so low."[19] With no fixed assets, production can follow the cheapest labor, the lowest taxes and tariffs, and the weakest environmental regulation. Today in Mexico, tomorrow in China, next month in Los Angeles. Instead of establishing a permanent workforce and standardized work schedules, companies contract out work on an as-needed basis. When consumer spending lags or there is a seasonal lull, labor is simply not hired, and production takes a break.

The benefits of flexible production for apparel manufacturers are plain to see: low start-up and overhead costs; cheap labor available on demand and with no long-term obligations; quick response time to fluctuations in fashion and consumer demand; and few regulatory restraints. Perhaps best of all, point out Bonacich and Appelbaum, the contracting system means manufacturers "do not need to invest a cent in the factories that actually sew their clothes."[20] The main benefit for consumers is also easy to identify: a constantly refreshed array of apparel options, including plenty of low-price imitations of high-end fashion items.

By contrast, the benefits for workers and the environment are much harder to discern. Insofar as the apparel industry provides work opportunities for those who would otherwise be unemployed, it is presumably better than no work at all. But the character and consequences of that work are troubling. Contract work is famously unpredictable. One never knows if or when one will have work. Trying to live a normal life in the midst of such economic and emotional instability is an enormous challenge, particularly when the wages, when they do come, are pitifully small. In addition, the labor is repetitive and the hours long. In the United States, most garment workers are pieceworkers, meaning they get paid not by the hour but according to the number of pieces they actually sew. Hourly wages are the norm in offshore production, but workers must meet steep daily quotas. In either case, the pressure to work as fast as humanly possible is intense.

Moreover, because manufacturers do not invest in factories, workplace conditions are often quite bad. We tend to think of sweatshops as a thing of the past or as a practice of other nations, and they were, in fact, largely curtailed as a result of New Deal legislation protecting workers. However, sweatshops are back in full force these days. U.S. Department of Labor surveys routinely find that upwards of 90 percent of apparel firms are in violation of health and safety standards, including disturbing numbers of life-threatening deficiencies. When business is moved offshore in search of an even more permissive regulatory environment, conditions for workers are typically worse.

What the apparel industry models with great clarity is the double-edged character of the new economy's highly touted practice of flexible production. The ability to respond quickly to the demands of the market or of giant retailers is the industry's great strength, allowing it to function quite profitably in a complex, fast-moving, and ever-changing world. The apparel industry's successful embrace of the contracting system, just-in-time production, and as-needed mobility make it a poster child for the new economy. For workers, however, the new economy looks an awful lot like the old one: boring, repetitive work in oppressive conditions for poverty wages.

The Limits of Flexibility. We might assume that when the "new" values of today's economy are considered from a white-collar worker's standpoint, they fare much better. Here again, however, we find there are two sides to the story. On the one hand, today's flexible economy offers unprecedented possibilities for the enhancement of white-collar workers' autonomy and quality of life. On the other hand, work for white-collar workers is increasingly "greedy"—outcompeting other institutions, including family, for workers' time and energy, and hence mitigating flexibility options. Moreover, new-economy terms like *flexibility, fluidity,* and *mobility* are sometimes simply euphemisms intended to rationalize and conceal negative characteristics of the economy like its increasing instability. That instability affects those at both the top and bottom of the work hierarchy.

Growing numbers of workers in today's contingent economy, including those with good educations and job readiness, wind up in America's fastest-growing job sector: the temp world.[21] Despite its nomenclature, for an ever-expanding portion of the population, this world is by no means temporary. In fact, given global capitalism's preference for short-term gain in the midst of constant change, the temp industry is likely to become a permanent feature of the new economic landscape. Ironically, even as work has supplanted family as the foundation for personal identity in our culture, the temp phenomenon

> The temp industry is likely to become a permanent feature of the new economic landscape.

appears bent on undermining work's identity-founding role. In the temp world, workers' individual identities are often invisible, nonexistent. The temporary worker's name is even disappeared in favor of the generalized moniker "the temp." Temps are only temporary, so why bother learning their names? Just ask "the temp" to make those copies or enter that data. In an economy of fluidity and mobility, who has time to learn each other's names or develop anything other than instrumentalist relationships? Certainly, companies that rely on temporary workers have mostly instrumentalist intentions toward them—favoring them over permanent employees because the company doesn't have to provide them with benefits and can, when layoffs are necessary, give them the ax without having to include them in company layoff statistics. While there are a few who love the freedom that temp work allows, the vast majority of temporary workers say they wish they had permanent employment. However, permanent employment is not a favored feature of the new economy.

For members of the professional and managerial class who find themselves out of work, today's "fluid" economy can be profoundly unsettling. Those whose identities have been closely tied to jobs find unemployment to be not only an economic blow but a personal and social humiliation as well. Some find solace and hope at upscale job clubs like Experience Unlimited in California, where yesterday's expectations about the work world meet today's sobering work realities.[22] In addition to phones, computers, printers, fax machines, and want ads, such agencies offer workshops to help members understand and adapt to the changed economy. A consistent theme is that predictability and continuity are hallmarks of a previous work era and should no longer be expected. Members are advised to downplay and even conceal their work histories and hopes for permanent employment. Instead, they are counseled to play up their flexibility and their comfort level with innovation, change, multitasking, and risk taking.

Work in the new economy, they learn, is not about stability or the long term. The new name of the game is the "project model"—that is, work organized around discrete, short-term projects instead of around the skills of a stable workforce. Because the skills needed for one project may not be the ones needed for another, workers will naturally come and go. Thus, one should prepare to be permanently on the job market rather than permanently employed. At Experience Unlimited, members work to reconstruct their identity and expectations to accommodate the new world. One reconstructive strategy is what members have dubbed "the

Thirty-Second Me"—a thirty-second self-presentation they can mobilize whenever and wherever a job prospect emerges, whether at a subway stop, in the checkout lane at the grocery store, or in the fellowship hall after church. One must be constantly on the watch for job leads, ready on a moment's notice to perform one's upbeat, flexibility-focused, innovation-embracing Thirty-Second Me. That kind of always-on job search is advocated by the following advice given in a pamphlet written for job seekers:

> Seek every opportunity to meet people. Don't wait until you actually walk into the meeting room to begin networking. If you arrive at the meeting place by car and notice a group of women in the parking lot, take the opportunity to strike up a conversation. "Are you going to the women's network meeting? Did you run into that traffic on the freeway?" Whether you are in the elevator, the ladies room, or waiting at the bar, start talking.[23]

If a downside of the new economy is its cultivation of invisible or superficial identities, then surely an upside is the new freedoms made possible by flexible capitalism. More and more of us can work from home for at least part of the workweek, or we can increase our time at home with our kids by working the night shift. "Flextime" promises some control over what hours we work, while "flexplace" lets us decide where we will work. Particularly for those who desire "family-friendly" work, these kinds of policies have the potential to ease work-family tensions and significantly improve quality of life. Interestingly, however, only a fraction of workers take advantage of them. Even those

Even those who can afford to spend less time at work generally do not.

who can afford to spend less time at work generally do not. Despite the professed desire of workers for greater flexibility with work and the increasing availability of such flexibility, relatively few white-collar workers use flextime and flexplace programs. Scholars usually point to organizational pressures to explain this paradox, and there can be little doubt that much of white-collar work culture encourages and rewards overwork. However, the anti-flexibility dynamics are not entirely institutional. In one study of the question, researchers found that even those who leave organizational structures and turn to independent contracting in order to have more control over their time nevertheless work as if they do not.[24] Many worry constantly that they will miss important business opportunities if they take time off of work, and many also experience feelings of guilt when taking time off. A similar story can be told about white-collar workers who take advantage of flexplace options to work from home. Thus, for today's white-collar workers, flexibility may promise greater freedom in relation to work, but in reality that freedom tends to be mostly rhetorical.

Where flexibility does come prominently into play for many white-collar workers is on the home front, where commitments to domestic work and family relations are stretched thin by contemporary work habits and pressures. Here we encounter another defining feature of today's world of work: the centrality of "emotional labor." More and more jobs today require voice-to-voice or face-to-face delivery of service, and workers of these jobs are often expected to deliver not only tangible goods such as a plate of food or directions to the nearest available exit but also intangible ones such as a spirit of hospitality, fun, or caring.[25] In addition to physical and intellectual labor, says sociologist Arlie Russell Hochschild, workers today must increasingly engage in emotional labor, practicing and polishing feelings and attitudes that make consumers feel good. Admittedly, the requirement that employees aim to please the customer is nothing new;

it's called customer service. However, Hochschild points out that more and more jobs depend for their success on interpersonal skills and the display of a prescribed set of emotions that must, to be effective, appear genuine. Consider, for example, flight attendants. Their job includes the delivery of tangible goods like safety information, in-flight beverages, and gate assignments, but at least as important is the pleasant mood they are responsible for creating. Flying involves a lot of noise and tension in a small, relatively uncomfortable space with restricted mobility; an important part of the flight attendant's job is to calm tensions, ease worries, and lift spirits. Toward that end, part of their job training focuses on the art of smiling—and not just superficial smiling, for as one airline boasts in a jingle, "Our smiles are not just painted on." Today, service sector workers like flight attendants are expected not only to do their job well but to *love* doing their job, because, says Hochschild, "the emotional style of offering the service is part of the service itself."[26]

To be able to exhibit a prescribed emotional disposition for a sustained period of time is not easy. One must manipulate one's feelings in order to achieve the expected mood and concomitant behaviors. Yet, in today's economy, the quality of service often *is* the product; "the product," in other words, "is a state of mind."[27] While such emotional labor is today part of the wage calculus—that is, workers are paid in part to be upbeat and friendly, or sincere and caring—what has not been adequately considered is the cost to workers. When even workers' feelings are controlled by employers, what consequences might there be for individual identity and integrity and, by extension, for authentic relationship with others?

Who Cares? For those who work in the rapidly expanding "care industry," taking care of those who are too young, too old, or too sick to care for themselves, emotional labor can be the main output of one's work. Because the majority of working-age Americans today work full-time jobs, the task of caring for the young, the old, and the infirm is increasingly contracted out to others. These others are paid to *care*, to be caregivers. But while they are mustering genuine care for someone else's loved ones, we might wonder about the impact on their own emotional lives and families. As Hochschild's investigation of the globalized nanny industry reveals, that impact can be devastating. Consider this experience of a Filipino woman working as a nanny in the United States:

> I love Ana more than my own two children. Yes, more! It's strange, I know. But I have time to be with her. I'm paid. I am lonely here. I work ten hours a day, with one day off. I don't know any neighbors on the block. And so this child gives me what I need.[28]

American parents are increasingly hiring immigrant nannies to care for their children while they are at work. These nannies are usually women who live in impoverished nations where work is scarce. Many, if not most, of these women are themselves mothers who migrate to the United States in search of work, leaving their children behind. Living in a strange country with few if any friends or relations, these women typically shower their American charges with the affection and caring they wish they could be giving their own children. Hochschild calls this heart-wrenching transfer of care a "global heart transplant"—the extraction of love from the Third World to the First, a contemporary version of nineteenth-century imperial extractions of Third World gold, rubber, and ivory. "Today," reflects Hochschild,

"In this sense," says Hochschild, "we can speak about love as an unfairly distributed resource—extracted from one place and enjoyed somewhere else."

"love and care become the 'new gold.'"[29] So, to support our work lives, we outsource the care of our children, creating decent work for someone else but at the same time producing a situation in which our child's care comes at the direct expense of another child's. "In this sense," says Hochschild, "we can speak about love as an unfairly distributed resource—extracted from one place and enjoyed somewhere else."[30] On the one hand, these workers freely choose to leave their families and migrate to another country. On the other hand, they are compelled by economic pressures beyond their control to try to provide for their loved ones, even if it means leaving them. This is globalization's underbelly, to be sure, and as both workers and employers, we are mired in it.

Many of those of us affluent enough to hire nannies belong to the small minority of Americans who find themselves beset by the challenges of overwork. Where increasing numbers of our fellow citizens are grappling with unemployment or underemployment, we few find our lives overwhelmed by work. When Juliet Schor and others talk about "the overworked American," they talk not about the majority but about this small but influential minority. For them—for us—work is sometimes wonderfully meaningful and fulfilling, and it is generally well enough compensated, but its grip on our lives is all out of proportion. Some of us clock in excess of sixty hours per week at the office; others of us bring our work home or find ourselves constantly

> We no longer work to live—we live to work.

preoccupied with it during "nonwork" hours. When given opportunities to work less or take a break, we frequently refuse. We pour ourselves into our work for a variety of reasons: it's enjoyable, gives us a sense of purpose, lets us actualize our talents or commitments, allows us to make a difference in the world, grants us access to a desired social or cultural world, is less stressful or more rewarding than home life, funds the lifestyle and consumption habits we desire. Regardless of what motivates our work, many of us seem to have lost perspective. As the saying goes, we no longer work to live—we live to work.

This chapter's sketch of work in today's globalized world is admittedly partial, but it does establish that contemporary practices of working take place within a complex historical context and are shaped by multiple fields of knowledge and power. More importantly, it reminds us that work is a deeply important personal and communal practice. It is a person-forming, world-constructing activity that is absolutely fundamental to human existence and community. Work can also be, at the same time, a personhood-destroying, world-unraveling activity. Because it is both these things, and because in this historical moment it is in powerful flux, it is incumbent upon Christians to consider what our tradition has to say about work. What wisdom about working can we offer the world? Are there particular moments in Christian history when the everyday practice of working elicited insight of special note or relevance for our situation today? To these questions we turn in the next two chapters.

2

biblical insights into working

The Bible is a primary touchstone for Christians regardless of where on the spectrum of identity and practice we find or position ourselves. We turn to this sacred text for spiritual sustenance, practical wisdom, and clues to our religious history and heritage. Therefore, to develop a Christian understanding of work, this chapter focuses on biblical insights into working. The chapter examines key biblical texts—presented against the backdrop of the wider Greek culture in which Christianity emerged, especially the historically influential writings of the philosophers Plato and Aristotle—for their work-relevant meanings and implications. We will see that the Bible does not speak in one voice when it comes to the topic of working but instead offers a diverse array of rich insights into this everyday practice that dominates so much of human life but about which we rarely reflect theologically.

The Greek Context

In the Greek culture in which Christianity emerged, the negative dimensions of work were powerfully articulated.[1] While the idea of work as a burden or curse is a relatively minor theme in biblical literature, it is the dominant view in many Greek texts. As such, it pervaded Christian culture for centuries.

In certain respects, the fifth-century B.C.E. Greek philosopher Plato paints a fairly positive picture of work. In *The Republic*, for instance, he depicts a harmonious and productive workforce in which each individual concentrates on one kind of work: "All things are produced more plentiful and easily and of a better quality when one man does one thing which is natural to him and does it at the right time, and leaves other things."[2] Rather than each person trying to do everything for him- or herself, Plato thought we should each specialize in one kind of work and then share the products of our work with others—not out of benevolence or solidarity but because sharing (or, rather, trading/exchanging) allows us as individuals to fulfill our own needs as efficiently as possible. A division of labor is necessary because "the husbandman will not make his own plough or mattock, or other implements of agriculture, if they are to be good for anything. Neither will the builder make his tools—and he too needs many; and in like manner the weaver and shoemaker."[3] A wide range of work and workers is required in a high-functioning society, proposes Plato, from shepherds and artisans to merchants and salespeople. Each has a duty to do his or her work conscientiously and well and to leave others to their own work. We are each suited to a particular kind of work, he thought, and that is the one work we should do.

Despite Plato's recognition of the necessity and value of diverse kinds of work, there is no doubt that in his ideal society, the highest form of work is performed by the philosophers, who dutifully exercise authority over those unfortunate enough to have to engage in more embodied forms of labor.

> In his ideal society, the highest form of work is performed by the philosophers.

These philosopher-kings are expected to rule benevolently, putting personal gain and caprice aside for the good of the whole city. However, what qualifies them for the power and authority they are granted over others is not their demonstrated virtue, nor their excellent work ethic or record, but their intellectual aptitude. Because they are the ones who can think abstractly and appreciate the world of ideas, they are destined to rule others. Plato places them, as philosophical thinkers, at the very top of the social hierarchy and grants them authority over everyone else (the "nonthinkers"). Thus, while Plato embraces a diversity of work roles and envisions harmonious relations among them, he constructs a thoroughgoing work hierarchy in which a certain kind of intellectual work has more power and status than anything else.

Another of Plato's key insights into work has to do with its social character. On the one hand, he was quite certain that self-interest and self-promotion are natural, unavoidable, and socially useful human tendencies. On the other hand, he believed work functions as a kind of antidote or countertendency to egocentrism. Through work, we attempt to meet our own needs and desires, and we promote and safeguard our own interests. However, for work to work, we also need others—others to join us in our work or to produce with their own labor the goods or services we need but cannot produce for ourselves. Work, then, is a naturally social endeavor. Without it, human community cannot exist. For Plato, work is not only an individualized survival strategy but also a form of sociality—a way in which we humans connect to each other and are schooled in reciprocity and social responsibility. Work, then, is a vital ingredient in justice. As Plato saw it, a healthy system of commerce requires and values the production of diverse goods and the contributions of diverse workers, each performing his or her own task and leaving others to do likewise. Although such a system is motivated primarily by self-interest, with the wise leadership of those equipped to lead (the philosophers), this system will aim toward the flourishing of all citizens rather than the happiness of only a few.

A final feature of Plato's thought that influenced Western notions of work was his contention that the intellectual realm of reality is metaphysically and morally superior to the material dimension or realm. For Plato and the schools of thought that developed in his wake, the realm of bodies and the work required to sustain them are merely shadows of the real. The body's work may be necessary for survival, and it may be a key ingredient of human sociality and community, but what *really* matters is the realm of ideas, spirit, and the mind. The less earthly and embodied something or someone is the more valuable, the more real. This dividing of reality into the material/bodily and the spiritual/intellectual, with the corresponding assumption of the moral and metaphysical superiority of the latter pair, is known as Platonic dualism, and it became a vital underpinning of Western thought and behavior for millennia. In terms of working, it offered powerful philosophical support for assumptions that physical labor and kinds of work that are more closely tied to human bodies and the earth are inferior to more intellectual or spiritual work.

In its directness and simplicity, Aristotle's articulation of the classical Greek antipathy toward "nonintellectual" work is even bolder than that of Plato, his teacher. Aristotle applauds the moral worth of the "active" life, but what he has in mind is contemplation: "thoughts with no object beyond themselves, and speculations and trains of reflection followed purely for their own sake."[4] What most people today think of as work is decried by Aristotle as morally suspect. The work of farmers, mechanics, and shopkeepers is characterized as "ignoble and inimical to goodness."[5] Why? Because such pursuits are a means to an end rather than ends in themselves. "Leisure" is far better than "occupation," says Aristotle, because it is intrinsically pleasurable. Where the worker labors in order to enjoy happiness once the work is done, the person of leisure enjoys it immediately. By "leisure," however, Aristotle does not mean indolence, rest, or even play. Rather, leisure is activity in conformity with virtue. Leisure time, then, is virtuous time. And the most virtuous activity of all is contemplation: "activity concerned with theoretical knowledge" or "the activity of our intelligence." Intellectual pursuit or contemplation breeds happiness, says Aristotle, because it is the exercise of "the highest possession we have in us." As additional evidence of contemplation's moral worth, Aristotle asserts that it can be performed more continuously than any other human endeavor, is "the only activity which is loved for its own sake," and is, moreover, the activity of the gods.

In Aristotle's valuing of contemplation above all else, we hear clear echoes of Plato's bifurcation of the material and the spiritual/ intellectual. Here again, the

> Intellectual pursuit or contemplation breeds happiness, says Aristotle, because it is the exercise of "the highest possession we have in us."

world of ideas is the most highly esteemed. Work is metaphysically and morally suspect because it is associated with embodied existence and the suffering of endless change and vulnerability. Those who wish to live as the gods do, to approximate immortality and perfection, eschew work. In keeping with his notion of god as the perfectly self-sufficient, unmoved mover, Aristotle applauds the fact that, unlike work, the activity of our intelligence does not depend on others but can be a self-sufficient practice. The intrinsically interdependent nature of work is for Aristotle a sign of its weakness, its immersion in the unpredictable, impermanent, and corruptible material realm.

For both Aristotle and Plato, the fact that work is necessarily embedded in a world of materiality, temporality, and interdependence means it is subject to all the indignities, vicissitudes, and corruptions of the finite realm. For the classical Greek tradition, the best that can be said of work is that it is a necessary evil, an unavoidable burden, an inconvenient requirement of earthly living. Even though Aristotle acknowledges that work's aim is the "external well-being" that

> For the classical Greek tradition, the best that can be said of work is that it is a necessary evil, an unavoidable burden, an inconvenient requirement of earthly living.

human existence requires, and Plato implies that work is a vital ingredient of human community, each is clear that the ideal world would not include work, unless by work we mean self-sufficient contemplation of eternal truths—in other words, a certain kind of intellectual work. Short of that, the best we can do is organize society so that those best suited for such pursuits are shielded as far as possible from the burdens, indignities, and moral compromise of physical labor. In Plato and Aristotle's day, the institution of slavery made it possible for some to escape from the curse of work. In our own day, we might acknowledge housekeepers, yard workers, and nannies, not to mention a highly stratified work world shot through with Platonic dualism, as contemporary ways of mitigating work's negativity and our immersion in its distasteful or inconvenient materiality.

In the classical Greek world, unemployment was a positive social virtue and a primary qualification for full citizenship. Today, by contrast, we tend to stigmatize the unemployed—assuming everyone should work—yet we reiterate Platonic dualism when we devalue (morally, socially, and monetarily) work that appears to be less intellectual, more physical. Aristotle believed that the natural order of the universe supported a stratified society in which some were "natural slaves," destined by their inborn incapacities for rational thought and contemplation to undertake the ignoble labors of physical work. Others were "naturally" suited for intellectual pursuits and the moral and civic leadership such pursuits allowed. We might wonder to what extent the work and pay hierarchies of our own day are undergirded by similar assumptions about the "natural" correlations between race/class/gender and work status.

Hebrew Scriptures

Compared with the tendency in the Greco-Roman world to view work with disdain, the biblical tradition offers a significantly more optimistic assessment of human work, including the everyday, embodied labors needed to sustain human life and community. Admittedly, it wasn't long before the strains of Platonic dualism were echoing loudly through the halls of Christian power, but in biblical texts, we encounter repeated affirmations of the theological and social worth of the kinds of work that Aristotle and other Greeks, as well as later Christians, seemed eager to impugn and avoid. As Douglas Meeks points out, the Bible assumes the perspective of the worker. Its point of view is most often not that of the boss or owner of the work but of the everyday worker.[6] As the following diverse examples demonstrate, the biblical corpus is by no means univocal in its portrayal of work. However, even as it sounds clear and urgent warnings about work's destructive tendencies, the weight of biblical consensus is easily on the side of work as an appropriate and valuable expression of both divine and human existence and community.

Workers in the Image of God.

In the beginning God created.

Genesis 1:1

God saw everything that God had made, and indeed, it was very good. And there was evening and there was morning, the sixth day.

Genesis 1:31

So God created humankind in God's image, in the image of God they were created; male and female God created them.

Genesis 1:27

[T]he LORD God formed man from the dust of the ground, and breathed into his nostrils the breath of life; and the man became a living being. And the LORD God planted a garden in Eden, . . . The LORD God took the man and put him in the garden of Eden to till it and keep it.

Genesis 2:7-8, 15

In biblical tradition, God works. God forms the world with patience, precision, deliberation, and imagination. God labors with words and ideas but also with God's hands and breath, embracing work that is both conceptual and embodied. Like a master craftsman whose care for the task runs deep, God pauses periodically to survey the work—to assess its progress and quality and to take pleasure in work well done. ("And God saw that it was good" [Gen. 1:10].) In its pace, God's laboring is steady and deliberate: "And there was evening and there was morning, the first day" (Gen. 1:5). Although stunningly prolific in terms of outcomes, this work is driven not by production quotas or profit goals but by a desire for self-expression, beauty, pleasure, diversity, and interrelation. God's labor brings order out of chaos; it shapes a world. God builds, forms, and plants. Contrary to widespread assumptions of *creatio ex nihilo*, "creation from nothingness," God does not create out of nothing. Instead, God takes what is at hand—the deep, the dust, the soil—and shapes it into something new and vibrant. As a worker, then, God is less hero or magician than midwife or artisan. God works not to exert dominance or achieve superiority but to make the world an inviting, diverse, and harmonious place. What we find narrated in the opening chapters of Genesis are the primordial labors

> God takes what is at hand—the deep, the dust, the soil—and shapes it into something new and vibrant.

of love. Work is constituted as both blessing and offering—necessary for life itself and, at the same time, site of profound creativity and connection.

According to the sacred text of Genesis, human beings are created in the image of God. As such, we can assume the centrality of work to human identity and action. We are workers just as God is. In the creation narrative of Genesis 2, we receive our job description. We are "to till and keep" the world God has created. Our job as humans, then, is to preserve and fortify God's good work. Our creativity and our labors are meant to support and proliferate God's primordial desire for a fecund and harmonious world. The same motivations and values that characterize God's work should presumably fuel ours as well: work as blessing and gift; work as a means to life-giving connection with others, including the nonhuman world; work as humanely paced and personally gratifying. We humans are workers. We were created to work as God works and to support God's great work of creating, loving, and sustaining the world in all its complexity and diversity.

Work as Curse.

By the sweat of your face you shall eat bread until you return to the ground, for out of it you were taken; you are dust, and to dust you shall return.

Genesis 3:19

Then the LORD said, "I have observed the misery of my people who are in Egypt; I have heard their cry on account of their taskmasters. Indeed, I know their sufferings, and I have come down to deliver them."

Exodus 3:7-8

Biblical tradition also recognizes that work can be a disfiguring curse, far from blessing or gift. Indeed, the relationship between God and Israel begins in a context of conscripted labor. In bondage to Egypt through forced labor, the Israelites cry out to God for liberation, and God hears and responds to their call. God acts decisively to free the people from exploitative work. The coupling of work and exploitation ignites divine resistance, holy outrage. What we humans distort, God acts to remake and redeem.

God acts decisively in the Garden of Eden narrative as well, and once again, work's burdensome quality is in the spotlight. However, instead of other humans imposing work-as-struggle, as happens in the Exodus story, it is God who does so. God mandates that work will require effort and even hardship. But why? According to the biblical narrative, because of human beings' refusal to live within limits, to accept our own finitude. God's ire is raised as Adam and Eve angle for godlike knowledge (and if knowledge is power, then power as well). Adam and Eve misunderstand what it means to be human: a wondrous and beloved creation of a relationship-seeking Divine and yet, at the same time, finite, limited, and clearly not divine. As Adam and Eve grapple with this foundational misrecognition and the inevitable disappointment of their infinite desire, their world—their horizon of meaning and understanding—undergoes a profound shift. The earthiness and earthliness that had been momentarily forgotten or rejected now come dramatically into focus. The world is no longer a boundless paradise. And human work is not only a fitting means for imitating God and even participating in God's creativity, but also and at the same time a temptation of sorts, a point of vulnerability. It is, we realize—but perhaps only in retrospect, in the painful wake of the overreaching—a primary means of self-exaltation, of distorted perspective, of losing our way in relation to God, of forgetting that we are dust and to dust we will return.

For Christians interested in the theological meanings of work, God's "cursing" of work in this biblical text is an Ash Wednesday moment. It calls us to account for the ways we overvalue work, abuse power in our work, exalt ourselves through work, and in so doing forget our proper role in relation to God and our neighbor. In response to these tendencies and habits, this text redefines work as a kind of discipline, a check on human pretensions to power, and a rejection of the myth of the self-made man. Even when we enjoy an ideal work situation ("paradise"), working still involves hardship and struggle. The story of God's "cursing" of human work suggests that the hardship dimension of work can serve not only as a rebuke of the human tendency toward work-idolatry and self-exaltation, but also as a reminder of who we as humans really are: daughters and sons of the dust, people of the earth, blessed with work to do.

Work without Meaning.

Then I considered all that my hands had done and the toil I had spent in doing it, and again, all was vanity and a chasing after wind, and there was nothing to be gained under the sun.

Ecclesiastes 2:11

What do mortals get from all the toil and strain with which they toil under the sun? For all their days are full of pain, and their work is a vexation; even at night their minds do not rest. This also is vanity.

Ecclesiastes 2:22-23

The author of Ecclesiastes (or, in Hebrew, Qoheleth) might as easily have been a contemporary low-wage worker as an ancient philosopher. The author's cynicism about work is familiar to anyone whose work is toil or who wonders about the meaning or value of his or her work. What is the point of laboring away at a low-status job for forty or more hours a week when one cannot even manage to provide oneself and one's loved ones with decent food, clothing, housing, and health care? For too many people today, the pursuit of "the American Dream" or even a modestly positive quality of life seems as pointless as "chasing after wind."

In city after city, living-wage analyses demonstrate that it is simply not possible to secure life's most basic amenities with a full-time minimum- or low-wage job. One can work long and hard, live frugally, and still not make ends meet. One can try one's best and still fail to live up to society's standards. What is the impact of this harsh reality on low-wage workers' self-esteem, on the quality of their relationships with family and friends, and on the vitality and depth of their civic, political, and religious engagement? When work isn't working, a pillar of personal and communal well-being crumbles, and we all suffer the consequences.

> **Finding meaning in work can indeed be like chasing the wind.**

Higher-wage workers may be better able to provide for life's necessities, but many can still feel the weight of the biblical author's searing indictment of work's futility: "Sure, I can pay the bills, but what *good* does my work really do?" Or: "No matter how hard I work, I can never seem to get ahead." Or: "I love my job, but there's got to be more to life." Finding meaning in work can indeed be like chasing the wind. When work fails to provide even the basics of life, the futility of that chase can be all the more deflating.

Work and Sabbath.

Thus the heavens and the earth were finished, and all their multitude. And on the seventh day God finished the work that God had done, and God rested on the seventh day from all the work that God had done. So God blessed the seventh day and hallowed it, because on it God rested from all the work that God had done in creation.

Genesis 2:1-3

Remember the sabbath day, and keep it holy. Six days you shall labor and do all your work. But the seventh day is a sabbath to the LORD your God; you shall not do any work— you, your son or your daughter, your male or female slave, your livestock, or the alien resident in your towns.

Exodus 20:8-10

Perhaps the most important insight into work in biblical tradition is that it must stop. No work is so urgent or necessary that it should occur without ceasing. No workers are so important *or* so unimportant that they should not have time away from work, time off the clock, time to rest and be rejuvenated. Chapter 4 will explore the contemporary implications of the Sabbath directive at some length. For now, we simply note that in both Hebrew and Christian scriptures, this directive occurs repeatedly. Biblical authors were clearly aware of work's tyrannical potential and of the consequent need for limiting or relativizing work. Despite the importance and grandeur of the divine work, God rests—and insists that we do likewise.

> Despite the importance and grandeur of the divine work, God rests—and insists that we do likewise.

Christian Scriptures

As the previous section underscores, God the worker is the lead character in the Hebrew scriptures. Contra the classical Greek tendency, God is portrayed not as an unmoved mover or leisured supreme being but as active, attentive, and industrious. In Christian tradition, God's nature and purpose are typically described using active language. God is creator, redeemer, and sustainer: God makes and invents, heals and mends, guides and inspires. For Christians, divinity is at least as much a verb as a noun. We may not know all the specifics, but we are confident that God is at work in the world—not only as a transcendent spirit or intellective force, but in and through bodies, matter, and all of creation. The positing by Jewish and Christian scriptures of a positive relationship between divinity and work is captured succinctly in the symbol of God the worker. This symbol signals a dramatic departure from Greek devaluations of work and from the disembodied, dispassionate divinity that buttressed the Greeks' view of work.

For Christians, the additional claim that God is an *incarnate* God means that regardless of anyone else's tendency to denigrate the material, earthly realm, we are called to see and proclaim God's vibrant and life-giving presence in the warp and woof of finite, fleshly, earthly existence. Moreover, as we consider Christianity's sacred texts about the incarnate divine, Jesus of Nazareth, we find in those texts rich and diverse examples of Jesus' and the early Jesus community's relationship to work.

Jesus' Work.

As Jesus passed along the Sea of Galilee, he saw Simon and his brother Andrew casting a net into the sea—for they were fishermen. And Jesus said to them, "Follow me and I will make you fish for people." And immediately they left their nets and followed him.

Mark 1:16-18

As Jesus was walking along, he saw a man called Matthew sitting at the tax booth; and he said to him, "Follow me." And he got up and followed him.

Matthew 9:9

In the gospel narratives, Jesus and his disciples abandon their ordinary work and lives to pursue and proclaim the in-breaking of God's kingdom. Jesus is a carpenter—a manual laborer who apparently leaves his trade behind to become an itinerant preacher and healer. His life is by no means one of moneyed leisure or ivory tower contemplation. Rather, Jesus and his disciples appear to be working-class people whose decision to abandon their livelihood probably puts them at risk of hunger and hardship. Instead of leaving behind the vulnerabilities and dangers of embodied existence, they sink more deeply into them. In his teachings and travels, Jesus is immersed in the considerable challenges and sufferings of people's everyday lives: illness, anxiety, disability, powerlessness, and loss.

True, he and his band of followers dispense with certain kinds or contexts of work: Simon and Andrew leave their nets, Matthew the tax booth, Jesus the workshop. But they remain rooted in the nitty-gritty realities of the workaday world. Even as they attempt to grasp and proclaim eternal truths, their feet remain firmly on the ground. Jesus and his friends do not abandon labor in order to take up leisure; they do not spend their time in undisturbed contemplation, nor are their material needs met by slaves or servants. For the early Jesus community, the strict bifurcations of Platonic dualism give way to a messier mix. Apocalyptic fervor and heavenly aspirations combine with this-worldly blessing, a kingdom within, and the healing energies of a caring touch. To be sure, Jesus' words bear wisdom and profundity, but he is no philosopher-king. Rather than being above the fray, he is in the thick of it.

If we were to imagine Jesus in today's work world, we would find him not in the boardroom or the corner office but among the low-paid or disenfranchised workers, offering them solace in their suffering and

> Jesus and his followers leave their previous labors behind not in order to escape work altogether but to embark on a new, shared work.

hope for a new day. Jesus would, no doubt, have a hard word to speak to today's fat cats and captains of industry, as well as the professional and middle classes who turn a blind eye to the hardships of the working poor and the unemployed. But along with this prophetic word would come a steady refrain of welcome and a heartfelt summons to participate in God's grace-filled kingdom of radical hospitality and inclusion. Jesus and his followers leave their previous labors behind not in order to escape work altogether but to embark on a new, shared work—a work that plunges them ever more deeply into connection with the disenfranchised and confrontation of the powerful.

Work in the Vineyard.

"For the kingdom of heaven is like a landowner who went out early in the morning to hire laborers for his vineyard. After agreeing with the laborers for the usual daily wage, he sent them into his vineyard. When he went out about nine o'clock, he saw others standing idle in the marketplace; and he said to them, 'You also go into the vineyard, and I will pay you whatever is right.' So they went. When he went out again about noon and about three o'clock, he did the same. And about five o'clock he went out and found others standing around; and he said to them, 'Why are you standing here idle all day?' They said to him, 'Because no one has hired us.' He said to them, 'You also go into the vineyard.' When evening came, the owner of the vineyard said to his manager, 'Call the laborers and give them their pay, beginning with the last and then going to the first.' When those hired about five o'clock came, each of them received the usual daily wage.

> He said to them, "Why are you standing here idle all day?" They said to him, "Because no one has hired us."

Now when the first came, they thought they would receive more; but each of them also received the usual daily wage. And when they received it, they grumbled against the land-owner, saying, 'These last worked only one hour, and you have made them equal to us who have borne the burden of the day and the scorching heat.' But he replied to one of them, 'Friend, I am doing you no wrong; did you not agree with me for the usual daily wage? Take what belongs to you and go; I choose to give to this last the same as I give to you. Am I not allowed to do what I choose with what belongs to me? Or are you envious because I am generous?' So the last will be first, and the first will be last."

Matthew 20:1-16

If Jesus were in the midst of *these* workers, he would no doubt get an earful! What kind of boss doles out pay with-out regard for the time card? How long will it be before this business (or this kingdom) goes out of business, thanks to ill-conceived generosity? Those who would make Jesus a poster boy for workers' rights and fair wages might likewise be con-founded by this strange parable in which the business own-er's unequal treatment of his employees appears to exemplify some kind of inscrutable divine wisdom.

If we allow the parable's summative comment, "So the last will be first, and the first will be last," to serve *as* a kind of summary, then we have an interpretive lens through which to view this narrative's discomfiting reversal of moral norms and workplace protocol. This lens prompts us to consider that the landowner's treatment of the vineyard workers may not be a mysterious game or arbitrary power play after all. Maybe, as with other parables Jesus told, it is a mind-blowing revalua-tion of values—an unsettling of long-held assumptions about what counts as work, who deserves to be paid, and how work ought to be organized in the first place. We note, for instance, that the laborers whom the owner of the vineyard hires at increasingly later hours of the day are waiting around in the marketplace because no one has hired them. In other words, they are ready to work, hoping for work. They spend the day looking for work, but no one is hiring. Perhaps what should rattle our moral cages in this scenario is not the boss's decision to pay all the laborers the same amount regardless of how many hours they clock, but rather a world in which there is apparently not enough work to go around and in which, nevertheless, only those who work are paid. The vineyard owner's inexplicable generosity pulls the veil of this work world aside, revealing its small-minded illogic. If an economic system produces or even requires unemployment, then what shame is there in being out of work? If some are ready and willing to work but cannot get hired, then should they go hungry, or be viewed as moral or social failures?

In the parable of the vineyard, the assumption of meritocracy—that those who get ahead in life are those who have earned it—unravels. All the laborers receive the same compensation, regardless of their output. Interestingly, the parable's audience is encouraged to view this inequity with understanding hearts. What the parable asks its audience to appreciate is apparently not productivity but something else: The willingness to work? The importance of work to human dignity and flourishing? The need for an economy that supports full employment?

Adding to this parable's provocative effect is the fact that the landowner's shocking "unfairness" does not square with the moral authority ascribed to him by the text and, we infer, by Jesus. Thus, the text's audience is invited to look more carefully at the situation: to acknowledge that only a few workers even had the chance to earn a full day's wages, and those few were no more or less deserving of work than any others. Their earnings, then, were a "gift" just as surely as was the pay doled out to those who worked fewer hours. Moreover, that any of the laborers were hired, whether at the start of the day or its close, was likewise a kind of gift. We have here a picture of work not so much as a right or entitlement but as a blessing.

What difference does it make when work is understood as a gift instead of as a burden, a necessary evil, an entitlement, or even a hard-won accomplishment? Work as gift—undeserved, yet freely given. How might such a view change our relationship to the fruits of our labor: to

> When understood as gift, work might not function as the moral and social plumb line it so often is today.

the money we are paid (or not paid), the authority we wield (or don't wield), or the status we achieve (or don't achieve) through our work? When understood as gift, work might not function as the moral and social plumb line it so often is today— a primary way of separating the righteous from the unrighteous, the worthy from the unworthy. Rather than inspiring ego-focused postures ranging from self-importance to self-loathing, work might instead cultivate hearts of thanksgiving and a desire to pay it forward by making one's work a gift to others. Biblical scholars identify the parable of the vineyard as one of "eschatological reversal" because it proposes that in God's space and time (i.e., God's kingdom or reign), the expectations and norms that characterize ordinary existence are turned topsy-turvy: "The last will be first, and the first will be last." True to form, this parable challenges us to rethink how work and workers are understood, organized, and valued.

Working for the Master.

"Therefore you also must be ready, for the Son of Man is coming at an unexpected hour. Who then is the faithful and wise slave, whom his master has put in charge of his household, to give the other slaves their allowance of food at the proper time? Blessed is that slave whom his master will find

at work when he arrives. Truly I tell you, he will put that one in charge of all his possessions. But if that wicked slave says to himself, 'My master is delayed,' and he begins to beat his fellow slaves, and eats and drinks with drunkards, the master of that slave will come on a day when he does not expect him and at an hour that he does not know. He will cut him in pieces and put him with the hypocrites, where there will be weeping and gnashing of teeth."

Matthew 24:44-51

If the parable of the vineyard calls typical work assumptions and norms into question, then this passage seems to do the exact opposite. Here, the Son of Man is characterized as a master, and the message appears to be that slaves should stay in their place, work hard, and avoid licentious behavior, or else suffer horrific consequences. On this reading, we would appear to have a forceful endorsement of traditional work hierarchies and protocols rather than a topsy-turvy reversal of norms. Even if we join most scholars in viewing the master-slave language as figurative rather than literal—as a metaphor conveying to the earliest Christians the need for moral vigilance in a situation of apocalyptic urgency—we must still contend with the fact that a key organizing principle of work in biblical times was the master-slave relationship. This particular passage features that relationship, with its top-down power dynamics, precisely because it was a fixture in Jesus' day.

Even so, a closer reading of the passage reveals a much less conservative message than we might initially assume. The fury of the master, we notice, is not directed to slaves per se but to the one slave who abuses his authority over the others. This slave has actually been given significant responsibility; he is to oversee the physical well-being of his fellow workers. If the slave fulfills this responsibility, he will be granted even more authority, becoming the caretaker of all the master's possessions. If, by contrast, he abuses his power and mistreats the other workers, then he will suffer the master's wrath.

What we appear to have here is a narrative about what we today would call the managerial class. And this narrative sounds a clear warning: If managers abuse workers, there will be hell to pay. All workers, even slaves, deserve to be treated humanely—for example, having food to eat and time in which to eat it. The cavalier use or abuse of power may have grave consequences, Jesus warns. According to this passage, the work itself is also to be respected. Even when supervisory eyes are looking in another direction, workers' obligation to the craft or task should keep them from squandering work time on personal indulgences or cruelties. Thus, a text that appears at first to underscore traditional workplace hierarchies is actually a warning against abuses of power in the workplace and an affirmation of both the dignity of workers and the importance of work itself for human living and community.

Rest from Labor.

Come unto me all you who labor and are carrying heavy burdens, and I will give you rest.

Matthew 11:28 (my translation)

This passage reminds us that the biblical Jesus is keenly aware of the toll work takes. Even in the best of circumstances, work is hard. As someone who spent most of his time with ordinary, working-class people, Jesus would have been attuned to the physical, emotional, and spiritual costs of work. In this passage, he speaks explicitly to workers, to those like the slaves or servants previously considered for whom work is more labor than vocation, more struggle than reward. Not only does Jesus recognize the existence of everyday laborers, seeing them and understanding the hardship and burden that work often poses, but he also calls them to himself for refreshment and rest. He ministers explicitly to workers *as* workers, laborers, those who toil and travail. And he invites them to put aside their burdens: the physical weariness and pain of manual labor, the emotional stress of overwork or underwork, the disappointment and shame of dashed work dreams, the worries about tomorrow's groceries, next month's rent, or an impending layoff. Jesus acknowledges the damage that working entails, and he offers a respite from it.

> The biblical Jesus is keenly aware of the toll work takes.

Notice that his promise is not to undo or destroy work's negativity. To be human is to work, and to work is both to create and to suffer. Jesus does not erase or ignore work's complexity or risk, but he embodies a deep and abiding concern for workers' well-being. He also reiterates the Sabbath wisdom that work must not come at the expense of justice; it is not its own end but is intended to enable human flourishing and contribute to God's work and glory.

The Work of Mary and Martha.

Now as they went on their way, he entered a certain village, where a woman named Martha welcomed him into her home. She had a sister named Mary, who sat at the Lord's feet and listened to what he was saying. But Martha was distracted by her many tasks; so she came to him and asked, "Lord, do you not care that my sister has left me to do all the work by myself? Tell her then to help me." But the Lord answered her, "Martha, Martha, you are worried and distracted by many things; there is need of only one thing. Mary has chosen the better part, which will not be taken away from her."

Luke 10:38-42

When Christians think about biblical views of work, the story of Mary and Martha is sure to come to mind. Interpretations of the narrative are legion. For our purposes, we might reflect briefly on the disparaging of work that seems to occur in the story as Jesus states unequivocally that Mary's choice to sit at his feet and listen to him is "better" than Martha's choice to spend her time running a household. Is he making the point that spiritual work is superior to physical work? Or that domestic labor is unimportant?

One aspect of the passage we sometimes overlook is its twofold mention of Martha's distractedness. Because of her workload and practices, Martha is apparently struggling to keep things in proper perspective, to maintain a healthy personal center or ground. Her work has a fragmenting affect; it "distracts" her from seeing the "better" parts of life and blunts her awareness of what is most important in life. Given the positive valuations of work found in other scriptures, it is unlikely that Jesus' criticism here is aimed at work per se. Rather, he seems concerned about the human tendency to overvalue work, to become so wrapped up in work that we fail to appreciate that it is not an end in itself but, rather, an avenue for self-expression and communal flourishing. Work is a worthwhile and necessary human endeavor, but it often includes a tyrannical dynamic—a tendency to take up all available space and time and to crowd out other good things.

It is easy to forget that work is what we *do*, not who we *are*. In the story of Mary and Martha, Jesus does not say or imply that household-sustaining work is worthless or unimportant. He does not shame Martha

> When work comes between us and our relationship to God or neighbor, then it is a problem.

for being committed to her work. He does, however, gently remind her that work's value is relative, and when work comes between us and our relationship to God or neighbor, then it is a problem. The overvaluing of work is just as dangerous as its undervaluing.

Another thing we might pause to consider is that in this famous biblical passage, Jesus turns the work assumptions of his day upside down. In taking her domestic duties seriously, Martha does what women in her day are expected to do. To those ensconced in that highly patriarchal culture, Jesus' chiding of Martha for doing exactly what her social role prescribes would come as a surprising flouting of convention. To claim that there is a "better" role for women than taking care of the household is still scandalous to some in today's world; imagine how it would have been received two millennia ago! The flip side of Jesus' gentle chiding of Martha is, of course, his affirmation of Mary's choice to take on the role of student. Women were typically not taught the Torah nor considered well suited to a life of the mind or spirit. That Jesus encourages Mary's desire to learn, particularly when it comes at the cost of the domestic tasks that are so clearly part of women's realm of responsibility, signals his willingness to defy traditional work roles. As in the parable of the vineyard, Jesus here unsettles reigning conceptions of work roles and valuations, this time challenging not the sacred cow of compensation but traditional assumptions of who is suited for socially valued kinds of work and who is not.

The Work of Paul.

"You know for yourselves that I worked with my own hands to support myself and my companions. In all this I have given you an example that by such work we must support the weak, remembering the words of the Lord Jesus, for he himself said, 'It is more blessed to give than to receive.'"

Acts 20:34-35

Now concerning love of the brothers and sisters, you do not need to have anyone write to you, for you yourselves have been taught by God to love one another; and indeed you do love all the brothers and sisters throughout Macedonia. But we urge you, beloved, to do so more and more, to aspire to live quietly, to mind your own affairs, and to work with your hands, as we directed you, so that you may behave properly toward outsiders and be dependent on no one.

1 Thessalonians 4:9-12

In these passages in which the apostle Paul counsels followers of Jesus on how to get along as an emerging church, work is presented as a positive attribute of Christian living and community. Work, says Paul, is a key to independence. Individuals who do not want to be a burden to others should labor in order to provide for their own needs. In a similar passage in 2 Thessalonians (3:6-13), Paul presents work as a positive antidote to idleness. Some of Jesus' followers were apparently abandoning work to wait for the second coming, but Paul makes it clear that work is a good and proper human enterprise that ought to be taken up by everyone who is able. "Anyone unwilling to work should not eat," declares Paul (3:10). While today's audience may readily connect this declaration to contemporary challenges such as "voluntary" unemployment and state-sponsored welfare programs, Paul's comment is clearly aimed in a different direction: toward those early Christians who are staying busy but who are not working. Paul admonishes those who fit this bill to take up work as a way to embrace independence and avoid idleness, which for Paul appears to include "empty" busyness. The purpose of work, suggests Paul, is not primarily to keep people busy but to enable independence and communal well-being. Work, then, is the proper activity of mature, responsible citizens.

In Paul's mind, work forms and demonstrates good character; thus, he encourages early Christians to embrace work as a vital ingredient of upright living. In the church communities Paul helps establish and lead, self-sufficiency is clearly valued, and work is explicitly named as a critical component of communal flourishing. Given the tendency in the wider Greco-Roman culture to view physical labor as the burden of the lower classes, it is notable that Paul singles out such work for special affirmation. Rather than being "ignoble and inimical to goodness" (Aristotle), working with one's hands is treated as a worthwhile aspiration and a valued accomplishment.

Not only does Paul affirm work as critical for the proper moral development of individuals and for communal well-being, he also suggests in the passages at the beginning of this section that work plays a positive role in the cultivation of the virtue of compassion. Work is not simply what we do for our own good and to serve those who are already in our circle of care and responsibility. It also has a centrifugal energy or intention that invites and allows its practitioners to expand their spheres of influence and relationship. Through our work and the commerce it enables, we reach beyond the bounds of self, family, and church to engage "outsiders." Work encourages us to "behave properly toward outsiders"—not merely treating them fairly but, Paul suggests, learning to love them as "brothers and sisters."

Even as he highlights the importance of his own hard work and self-sufficiency, Paul emphasizes that one of work's vital attributes is that it allows for provision for the weak. His enthusiastic endorsement of work does not, then, come at the expense of the recognition of work's limits. As important as it is for individual development and community well-being, work simply does not work for everyone. There are always those in need of the solace and provision that the work of others can offer, and Paul states explicitly

> Through our work and the commerce it enables, we reach beyond the bounds of self, family, and church to engage "outsiders."

that Christians are to use their work for such care of the weak. Paul is also explicit in his use of the language of gift to describe the life-enhancing possibilities of work. Those who make of their work an offering to others are blessed indeed.

Treatment of Workers.

Listen! The wages of the laborers who mowed your fields, which you kept back by fraud, cry out, and the cries of the harvesters have reached the ears of the Lord of hosts.

James 5:4

This work-relevant passage comes from the short but fiery book of James. In the fashion of the Hebrew prophets, the author excoriates "the rich" whose wealth and status come at the expense of the poor. Our author means this quite literally: The owners of industry, he charges, have defrauded their workers—impoverished them by unjustly garnishing their wages. And the workers apparently have no judicial recourse.

Sadly, this appears to be a time-honored situation. We might think, for example, of undocumented workers in our day whose employers refuse to pay them their just due or who place them in dangerous work situations, knowing full well that these workers have limited access to social support and justice systems. Or we might recall an industry-leading company found guilty of routinely forcing employees to work overtime without pay, at times locking them into buildings so they could not leave when their official shift was over. Wage theft is by no means an antiquated practice but is, rather, a standard part of many workers' lives and an accepted MO of some companies.

This kind of exploitation of workers' vulnerabilities and labor is precisely what the author of James rails against.

According to this passage, God is well aware of labor's unjust treatment. The cries of workers have already reached God's ears. The question is whether the privileged have ears to hear as well.

Faith and Work(s).

For we hold that a person is justified by faith apart from works prescribed by the law.

Romans 3:28

What good is it, my brothers and sisters, if you say you have faith but do not have works?

James 2:14

An overview of key biblical insights into working would not be complete without some attention to the great faith-versus-works debate. Paul is the key protagonist here, with his famously influential claim that "works" have no bearing on salvation. Taking aim at his own experiences as a Pharisaic Jew in first-century Palestine, Paul argues that the good news of Jesus Christ is that we humans no longer have to bear the burden of our own salvation by working to fulfill myriad devotional, dietary, and behavioral obligations. Our salvation is a free and generous gift from God, he avows, not something we can accomplish through our own well-intended piety. When it comes to ultimate matters, our work is worthless. Putting aside the question of the accuracy of Paul's interpretation of his own Jewish tradition, we might note his convert's zeal—the dramatic contrast he draws between his past life and religious worldview and the new space he inhabits as a follower of Jesus. To embrace the good news of Jesus the Christ means for him a wholesale turnaround to a new way of seeing and being, a rejection of what came before—that is, a works-focused theology.

Looking back on Paul's theology with twenty-first-century eyes wide open to the centuries of terror inflicted on Jews by overzealous Christians, we can appreciate the dangers of his bifurcated theology—the ease with which his sincere disillusionment with his former religious identity developed into an equally sincere theology that pitted the new against the old, us against them, faith against works—and the ease with which this bifurcated theology fueled horrific prejudice and eventually, with opportunity and means, deadly violence. It is impossible to know to what degree Paul's antipathy toward "works" was motivated by his efforts to redefine himself over against his former community and tradition, but we can at least acknowledge the complex energies at play in his anti-works theology.

We might also contend that what Paul means by "works" is not the same as what we in this book mean when we consider work and working. We have not, after all, proposed that work is a means to salvation, nor that it necessarily exists in tension with faith, grace, or other terms of religion. On second thought, however, we should probably acknowledge that for many people in today's world, work does have an almost sacred value insofar as it enables participation in consumer society. As we noted in chapter 1, work is perhaps the most pervasive identifier of personal worth that we have these days, at least in developed nations. Without work, we may be hard pressed to know who we are either as individuals or as social beings. Given this reality, Paul's contention that "works" are overvalued might be especially relevant for us today, a possibility we have already noted and will return to in chapter 4. For now, it is important to recognize that in addition to various biblical passages in which Paul endorses the merits of hard work and physical labor, he also develops a theological vision in which "works" are the primary obstacle to be overcome. However, in this context, what Paul seems to mean by "works" can be boiled down to human effort itself, which means we cannot simply equate "works" with "work."

We run into a similar complexity when it comes to the enthusiastic endorsement of "works" articulated in the biblical book of James. When the author, whom we'll call James, insists on the vital importance of works for Christian flourishing, he clearly does not have in mind a person's occupation or livelihood. Rather, he means the everyday embodiment of our religious identity and commitments. James does not refute the necessity of faith for salvation but insists that unless that faith is enfleshed, it has no life. Works, then, refer to the varied ways we body forth our faith. In them, we respond affirmatively to divine grace. Although James is not referring explicitly to work as livelihood or occupation, his insight into the proper role of works in Christian living may yet be profoundly relevant for considerations of work and working—a possibility to be explored in chapter 4.

> Our work is both God's gift to us and our gift to others.

For now, we will conclude our consideration of key biblical texts on work by acknowledging that, for all their differences, the theologies of Paul and James are amenable to an understanding of work in terms of gift. Our work is both God's gift to us and our gift to others. Where Paul emphasizes God's gift, James highlights ours. A proper understanding of work requires both.

Conclusions

Even a cursory review of key biblical texts related to working yields the recognition that although the biblical tradition provides no single portrayal or "theory" of work, working is nevertheless depicted in a far more positive light than in the writings of ancient Greek philosophers like Plato and Aristotle, whose ideas shaped Western civilization in powerful and enduring ways. On the whole, the biblical tradition treats work as a necessary and worthwhile endeavor—suitable not only for human beings but also for God. Work is depicted as a means of survival, to be sure, but also as a primary means of creativity, self-sufficiency, interdependence, and the cultivation of compassion.

One of the first things we learn about human beings in the Bible is that we were put on earth to preserve and fortify God's good work. That human beings are constituted as workers in the Garden of Eden means our paradisal condition *includes* work. Work is not, then, primarily a curse but a life-sustaining vocation. As humans, we are called by God to preserve and nurture a fecund and harmonious world. No matter what our particular work is, that fundamentally human vocation remains. Even when work is toilsome, boring, alienating, or a site of disfiguring self-exaltation, as biblical tradition acknowledges it can be, the potential for it to be a blessing—a gift from God and for others—abides. It is the Christian's job to try to actualize that potential, receiving the gift of God's work in the world with grateful hearts and making of his or her own work a gift to others, all the while remembering that we are dust, and to dust we will return.

3

insights from christian tradition

When we leave the Bible behind and turn to the rest of Christian tradition for insights into working, we find a multitude of texts, ideas, and movements we might draw upon. An author's challenge in a short book of this nature is to select a few key moments of great influence or particular interest. This chapter lifts up three such moments for extended consideration: the Protestant Reformation, the nineteenth-century Social Gospel movement, and Catholic social teachings. Each of these distinctive strands of Christian history and tradition offers fascinating and influential insight into the complex nature and theological import of working. Each also poses still-relevant questions and challenges for today's world of work.

The Protestant Re-formation of Work: Medieval Motivations

In the previous chapter, we saw that the Bible's relatively positive valuation of work came into focus for early Christians against the backdrop of the work-disparaging tendencies of the Greek worldview. Biblical texts contain plenty of warnings about how we humans distort and overvalue work, turning it into a means of self-exaltation or exploitation of others. Yet, compared with powerful messages of work's negativity, such as those articulated by Plato and Aristotle, it is remarkable that biblical messages about work are as positive as they are. It is remarkable, moreover, that the Bible assumes the perspective of workers instead of philosophers or kings. We cannot appreciate the Bible's distinctive take on working without some understanding of the context in which it would have been heard and experienced by our early Christian forebears.

Similarly, Reformation writings about work took shape in a particular context and can perhaps be best understood as a response to certain elements of that context. Scholars of work often depict Martin Luther and his fellow Reformers as ushering in a new era not merely for the church and many of its doctrines and practices but also for Western notions of work.[1] They did so in response to the prevailing attitude toward work of the European Middle Ages. In spite of biblical revaluations of work, medieval Christian attitudes toward work tended to echo the negativity of the Greek worldview. Bodies were generally viewed as a hindrance to salvation—a source of temptation and a constant reminder of one's corruptibility and finitude, of how far from God one really was. Pope Innocent III's (d. 1216) characterization of the human body typifies this view: "Man was formed of dust, slime, and ashes: what is even more vile, of the filthiest seed. He was conceived from the itch of the flesh, in the heat of passion and the stench of lust, and worse yet, with the stain of sin. . . . He will become food for the worm which forever nibbles and digests; a mass of rottenness which will forever stink and reek."[2] In a cultural context in which this sort of vitriol against the body and its natural processes was commonplace, we can understand how work, whose first aim was to meet the needs of the body, was assumed to have little religious value. It was part of the earthly realm, after all, while God and church participated in a higher, spiritual reality.

Those whose work was of a more spiritual or intellectual nature were widely assumed in the medieval West to be closer to God and less vulnerable to worldly temptation and sin than those whose labor was more embodied or earthly. Thus, priests and monks, along with the occasional statesman, stood at the top of the social and theological hierarchies of the day. Twelfth-century political philosopher John of Salisbury's depiction of medieval social roles and power is a classic example. Using the human body as a metaphor, John identifies the body's head with the "higher order" intellectual and spiritual work of church and state leaders, while the feet are associated with "the humbler offices"—specifically, "the manifold forms of getting a livelihood and sustaining life." John unapologetically notes that most people are, in fact, feet: "All these different occupations are so numerous that the commonwealth in the number of its feet exceeds not only the eight-footed crab but even the centipede."3 Just as the feet are naturally at the bottom of the body, so too is the "humbler" work of the masses naturally at the bottom of the social and vocational ladder.

> In monastic culture, the tendency was to view spiritual work as the proper human occupation and physical work as valuable mainly as a form of spiritual discipline.

In the medieval West, Aristotle's privileging of contemplation as the human ideal was alive and well in monastic culture, where the tendency was to view spiritual work as the proper human occupation and physical work as valuable mainly as a form of spiritual discipline—a means for taming desire, curtailing the ego, and mortifying the flesh. Even so, by the late Middle Ages, fewer and fewer monks performed physical work, leaving the lower classes to provide for the body's needs and focusing their time and energy instead on performing spiritual disciplines for the benefit of the wealthy. Ironically, wealth itself was generally viewed in ecclesial culture as a stumbling block. Despite the church's immense holdings of property and purse, it advocated poverty as a spiritual discipline and warned about the moral dangers of money. Looking back on this situation, we can see that the monastic renunciation of worldly possession and pursuit, which was lifted up as the ideal attitude toward earthly existence, not only enriched the church's coffers but also gave theological credence to the rigid class stratifications of the day by suggesting that poverty was a good and noble thing. Thus, while the social and ecclesial body's "head" enjoyed high-value work and the wealth and power it bestowed, the multitudes of "feet" who undertook the necessary work required to sustain life and community had to suffer not only socially devalued work roles and the poverty they bestowed but also the burden of thinking their poverty and hardship were intended by God.

The Protestant Re-formation of Work: Martin Luther

Into this socially and theologically complex milieu came Martin Luther, struggling monk and vitriolic ecclesial critic, whom scholars often identify as progenitor of the modern notion of work as vocation. As the well-known story goes, Luther found himself as a young but devoted monk tortured by uncertainty about the ultimate value of his heartfelt religious observances and monastic practices. What if they weren't enough? What if, despite his best efforts to be a good and faithful Christian and an exemplary monk, he still fell short of salvation? Out of this cauldron of existential doubt and theological terror, and flavored with no small dose of antiestablishment and anti-Jewish venom, came Luther's signature conviction that human works count for

"Though you were nothing but good works from the soles of your feet to the crown of your head, you will still not be righteous or worship God or fulfill the First Commandment."

nothing when it comes to matters of salvation. "Though you were nothing but good works from the soles of your feet to the crown of your head, you will still not be righteous or worship God or fulfill the First Commandment," he declared.[4] Contrary to common belief and church canon, good works have no bearing on salvation, insisted Luther. We are saved by God's grace alone, which we accept by faith alone. Even the heroic religious observances of cloistered monks cannot secure salvation.

But if this was so, then suddenly the old ways of thinking about work no longer made sense. Suddenly, no one's work could be deemed more valuable than anyone else's. The strict dichotomy between spiritual or intellectual work and earthly or embodied work began to crumble, at least in theory. As Luther's theological vision developed, he articulated a cosmology or worldview in which there are two realms or worlds: the heavenly kingdom and the earthly kingdom. Matters of salvation pertain to the heavenly realm, and nothing we humans do on earth can manipulate that realm. God's grace abounds, and we can accept that grace or reject it, but our response does not change the fact that it is real and freely offered to all. We cannot earn God's favor, no matter how holy we try to be or how hard we work. The heavenly kingdom is, quite simply, beyond our control. Our work doesn't matter there.

But the earthly kingdom is another matter altogether, according to Luther. There we can have an impact. There our work matters. Through our good work(s), we have an impact not on God but on ourselves and our neighbor. Our work may have no bearing on ultimate matters of salvation, but it is a key to the moral content and quality of our earthly lives. Works such as fasting and laboring help discipline the body, says Luther, bringing it into alignment with the mind and spirit and purging it of "idleness" and "evil lusts." As such, work and works are vital to the individual's moral development. In addition, they are the means through which we serve our neighbor: "A man does not live for himself alone in this mortal body to work for it alone, but he lives also for all men on earth; rather, he lives only for others and not for himself."[5] For Luther, a primary axis around which work's value turns is service to others. The kind of work we do, the esteem with which the larger society views our work, the monetary value of our work—none of these things really matter. What matters is that we serve others with our work. Suddenly, the whole framework for understanding and valuing work is redefined.

In one fell swoop, Luther both demotes and promotes work. On the one hand (the kingdom-of-heaven hand), work is utterly useless, and our attempts to exalt it laughable. On the other hand (the kingdom-of-earth hand), work is the way we love our neighbor; it is how we obey half of the Great Commandment. God calls us to serve others, and we do that in our work. But that service, that work, earns us not one iota of God's grace.

Luther's concept of vocation includes another complexity. A vocation, he says, is God's call to us to love our neighbor through whatever work our "station" in life gives us. In other words, and in contrast to today's popular understanding, Luther does not define a vocation simply as a specific job or kind of work to which God calls us. Rather, a vocation is work

> A vocation is work in response to God's call to serve others.

in response to God's call to serve others. The distinction here is subtle but important. According to Luther, our work is a vocation if, and only if, we use it to serve our neighbor. Thus, God's call pertaining to work has primarily to do with the outcome or beneficiary of our labor, rather than with the specific kind of work we undertake. Contrary to Greek and medieval Christian assumptions, what matters most is not the spiritual or intellectual content of our work, but whether or not the work benefits others. The social implications of this view of vocation are dramatic. After all, *any* kind of work can serve others. If service is the criterion, then "high-class" work is no better than "low-class" work. Luther's concept of vocation, if taken at face value, seems to equalize work roles and to relativize their connections to power, status, and money—in theory, at least.

In reality, Luther did move boldly in the direction of abolishing the status hierarchies associated with work in his day. He famously argued that the work of popes, priests, and monks is no more religiously efficacious than any other kind of work. If human works, including ecclesial ones, cannot achieve salvation, then the playing field is leveled. Luther's "priesthood of all believers" assumes this leveling in its claim that we all have equal access to God. As he attempted to deflate the status and theological hubris of those at the top of the work ladder, Luther also sought to endow what John of Salisbury called "the humbler offices" with new value. Luther claimed that mundane jobs—the kind that Aristotle decried as "ignoble and inimical to goodness"—were at least as laudable as those of priests, monks, and popes:

> It looks like a great thing when a monk renounces everything and goes into a cloister, carries on a life of asceticism, fasts, watches, prays, etc. . . . On the other hand, it looks like a small thing when a maid cooks and cleans and does other housework. But because God's command is there, even such a small work must be praised as a service of God far surpassing the holiness and asceticism of all monks and nuns.[6]

If the standard is service to others, then regardless of the kind of work we do, we can each enjoy work as vocation.

Using the notion of kenosis, or self-emptying, to describe the proper attitude toward work, Luther acknowledges that although the Christian is "free from all works, he ought in this liberty to empty himself . . . and to serve, help, and in every way deal with his neighbor as he sees that God through Christ has dealt and still deals with him." From a grace-filled heart "flow forth love and joy in the Lord," says Luther, "and from love a joyful, willing, and free mind that serves one's neighbor willingly and takes no account of gratitude or ingratitude, of praise or blame, of gain or loss." Offering "our body and its works" freely to our neighbor, we "each should become as it were a Christ to the other, that we may be Christs to one another and Christ may be the same in all."7 According to Luther, when we do our best work and serve others in our work, we participate in God's ongoing providence. No matter what our station in life might be, we can use our work to serve our neighbor and glorify God.

> We "each should become as it were a Christ to the other, that we may be Christs to one another and Christ may be the same in all."

Here we might pause to consider what Luther means by this talk of one's "station" in life and what the implications are for his rethinking of work as vocation. For all its equalizing intention and potential, Luther's revaluation of work seems to stall out because of a key assumption: that our "station" in life is ordained by God and is hence a good and rightful part of God's plan for the universe. While in some ways Luther defied the norms and practices of his day, in others he was thoroughly a product of his time. His endorsement of a static, hierarchical world of work is one such example. Luther not only argued that the work role or "station" into which we are born is the one in which we should die, but he strengthened the theological justification of this view by claiming that our current station in life is God's intention for us and should be honored as such. The work hierarchy in the earthly kingdom is established by God, he argued, as a way to provide for diverse human needs. Our duty is not to try to change our station or improve our lot in life but to accept the status quo as God's will. In this theological scenario, dissatisfaction with one's station in life is rebellion against God.

Luther's social conservatism is hardly surprising, given the time in which he lived—a time when social hierarchies and rigid divisions of labor were taken for granted as the natural order of things and when social mobility as we know it today was simply inconceivable. Nevertheless, he left us with a highly paradoxical concept of vocation. On the one hand, the janitor's work is as valuable and praiseworthy as the lawyer's or the pope's. What matters is not the kind or social status of our work but whether or not we serve our neighbor through our work. If so, then traditional work hierarchies and their systems of reward and entitlement appear to lose their footing, while prospects for a more egalitarian organization and valuation of work improve and find fresh theological support. On the other hand, however, God has ordained that wherever our birth lands us in the work and social status hierarchy is where we are intended to be and where, therefore, we should happily (or at least dutifully) remain. If work's social status truly does not matter, then we should be content to remain where we are, even if that means low pay and social esteem, oppressive work conditions, or any number of other indignities. Luther's theology of work cuts both ways. It both justifies and resists profound stratifications of power, money, and social status. What Luther's heavenly kingdom seems to dissolve—that is, entrenched work hierarchies and systemic power differentials—his earthly kingdom depends upon.

Lest we cavalierly dismiss Luther's concept of vocation as fatally flawed due to the contradiction (paradox?) at its root, we should probably take a hard look at our own work environments and practices. Do they square with our theologies, our convictions about God and human dignity? Luther's premodern assumptions about the permanently stratified nature of social existence and work roles may strike us today as naive or elitist, but even within Luther's own thought world, these assumptions existed side by side and were at least partially relativized by his passionate insistence that the proper end of work is service to others, care of those in need. The idea of permanent stations in life and work may strike twenty-first-century Christians as morally offensive, but Luther would similarly judge our tendency to think of our work in proprietary terms—as our own property to do with as we please, as private rather than communal goods. We might also wonder whether today's social stratifications along lines of income, race, and work roles are any less permanent than were Luther's stations. Where Luther identified God as the source and validation of work hierarchies, we look to the market as final arbiter of value. In both cases, a highly stratified work world is experienced as a permanent and incontestable feature of the way things are.

The Protestant Re-formation of Work: John Calvin

John Calvin, another well-known Protestant Reformer, also employed the language of vocation to talk theologically about work, and like Luther, he defied tradition in emphasizing the importance of every person's work, not just the work of those with high social status. Calvin's understanding of work as vocation differs in crucial ways from Luther's, however, and eventually had a profound impact on Western understandings and practices of work.

"The Lord bids each one of us in all life's actions to look to his calling," says Calvin.[8] Our calling from God, our vocation, can ground and secure us in the face

> "The Lord bids each one of us in all life's actions to look to his calling."

of the "great restlessness" and "fickleness" that characterize human nature. God "has appointed duties for every man in his particular way of life," says Calvin, and these duties we know as "callings." Each of us is called by God to a particular way of life, a particular kind of work, and that work functions as a "sentry post" of sorts, helping us know who we are and what we should do with our lives. Indeed, our calling from God should be "the beginning and foundation of well-doing," according to Calvin. It should be the "straight path" that guides our life, the axis around which everything else turns, the principle that guides and orders our daily lives.

Departing from Luther, Calvin proposes that the particular work to which persons are called is determined not so much by our station in life as by our gifts. Just as the body's varied parts play different roles (eyes for seeing, feet for walking), so people are variously equipped by their God-given talents and abilities to do different kinds of work. Our gifts determine our station in life, says Calvin, which means that part of our challenge as Christians is to find a station in life where our gifts can be used for the common good. Calvin's world is a more malleable one than Luther's, thanks to dramatic economic, technological, and political changes that took place in Europe at the time, and the consequences for work are profound. Instead of a static social universe imposed by God in which one's calling or vocation is predetermined and fidelity to that singular calling or vocation is a civic and religious duty, Calvin gives us a world in need of transformation, a world in which each person must discern a calling that will contribute to social change and the world's renewal. In this context, Christians should look to their God-given talents for vocational guidance, and they should choose work that both employs their gifts and moves society toward conformity with the word of

God. However, if a time comes when one's chosen work no longer serves that larger theological end, or a different vocational path would allow for greater alignment with that end, then it is one's religious duty to pursue a new work. Gone, then, are the rigid social structure and corresponding work roles that undergirded Luther's notion of vocation. Calvin's ideal society is admittedly still a highly differentiated one; after all, the body is not a body without its varied parts and functions, without lesser parts and greater parts working together for the good of the whole. So, too, does the social body require a diversity of work roles functioning harmoniously for the sake of the whole. But instead of those roles being determined by a station in life one did not choose and from which one cannot stray, Calvin says a person's talents and abilities are what make him or her suited for one kind of work rather than another.

What a gifts-focused notion of vocation allows and even encourages is social mobility. I may be the daughter of a housekeeper, but if I have the talent to become an engineer, then that is what I can pursue. According to Calvin, in fact, I am squandering my gift and disobeying God if I do *not* pursue that calling. "All our actions are judged" by God on the basis of their conformity to our calling, he insists. So as Christians, we are duty-bound to pursue our calling, and there we are to remain. Indeed, "it is not lawful to exceed [the] bounds" of our calling, Calvin admonishes. Less threateningly, he suggests that a life directed toward one's calling is a well-ordered, harmonious, and satisfactory life.[9] Pursuing our calling means living as we were created to live; it means doing what God intends us to do.

> Pursuing our calling means living as we were created to live; it means doing what God intends us to do.

Those whose work is laborious or socially despised can take comfort in the knowledge that "the burden was laid upon

[them] by God." With that consolation in mind, says Calvin, "each man will bear and swallow the discomforts, vexations, weariness, and anxieties in his way of life" with fortitude and contentment. After all, when one's work is ordained by God, then "no task will be so sordid and base . . . that it will not shine and be reckoned very precious in God's sight."[10] As with Luther's stations, contemporary readers may find themselves disturbed or put off by Calvin's theologically inspired fatalism regarding work roles and inequities. For those at the top of the work heap, the expectation that workers will dutifully and steadfastly fulfill predetermined vocational roles may be palatable enough, but for those at the bottom, it can sound like a sinister rationalization of social injustice. In Calvin's scenario, however, where God-given callings correspond to God-given gifts and abilities, work is both duty and self-actualization. That we are called by God to do a particular work and to do it energetically and well is for Calvin a wonderful blessing, for without such a centering force, we would surely be tossed to and fro by life's vicissitudes or lured into immorality or sloth. Thanks to God's bestowal of a calling or vocation, our life can have direction and purpose. For Calvin, work understood as calling or vocation is at the very center of Christian identity and discipleship.

Like Luther, Calvin emphasizes that our calling or work should serve the common good. As he says, "All the gifts we possess have been bestowed by God and entrusted to us on condition that they be distributed for our neighbors' benefit."[11] As beneficiaries of God's good gifts, we are to offer our gifts to others. In the Reformation tradition of Luther and Calvin, our work is not ours but God's, and we offer that work back to God by serving our neighbor with it. With eyes wide open to the fact that no human work can earn salvation, the Reformers nevertheless effect a robust reversal of the Greek-medieval synthesis on work, embracing work as vocation or calling—the proper human response to divine grace and providence and the primary means through which we love and serve our neighbors.

For Calvin and his followers, work takes on an even more exalted role. Just as God works ceaselessly to sustain the universe, so should we work ceaselessly as well. We were created in God's image, after all. Contrary to the god of the philosophers for whom contemplation is the highest good, Calvin praises the virtues of the active life and suggests that God favors work over contemplation. Calvin's embrace of work as a religious duty and virtue was echoed by Christians across Europe and the New World. When William Perkins, one of the great English Puritans, speaks of work in terms of vocation or calling and boldly identifies "idleness and sloth" as the two "damnable sins," he is squarely in Calvin's work lineage.[12] For Perkins and other influential Calvinists like John Winthrop and John Cotton, the performance of good work(s) is a sign of pious living and religious seriousness. Through work, one is believed to participate in God's providential care of the universe. Since God calls us to work and even assigns us the particular work for which we are best suited, unemployment tends to be viewed by the Calvinists as a moral failure, a rejection of God's plan for our lives. Hard work, by contrast, is a

> Through work, one is believed to participate in God's providential care of the universe.

religious duty, and the acquisition of wealth that comes from its embrace is seen as the proper fruit of pious living, a sign of God's grace.

Even as we identify the ways in which Reformation notions of work depart dramatically from the work-negativity of the Greek/medieval synthesis, we should not lose sight of the Reformers' enduring awareness of the reality and pervasiveness of human sin. Work may be a religious duty for Christians, and those who work hard may rightfully enjoy social esteem, material prosperity, and even divine blessing, but we humans are always and everywhere vulnerable to the temptations and distortions of pride and self-love. Although the Reformers themselves did not problematize work in quite this way, their theologies nevertheless remind us that as with any other part of human experience, work can become an idol, a fetish, a diversion from God and neighbor. When we forget that work is a gift from God, when our work serves narrow individual goods instead of the common good, or when we act as if we can work our way to holiness or happiness, we misunderstand at a profound level the proper goodness and function of work.

> As with any other part of human experience, work can become an idol, a fetish, a diversion from God and neighbor.

Despite this sobering reminder of the human tendency to think too highly of ourselves and our efforts, what is most remarkable about Reformation conceptions of work is how different they are from Greek and medieval understandings. In only a few pages, we have moved from Aristotle's world, in which work is a necessary evil and unemployment is a privilege, to a world in which work is a divine calling and a primary means of participating in God's plan for creation. We have moved from the Christian Middle Ages, where poverty was an important spiritual practice and wealth was a stumbling block to faithful living, to the Protestant Reformation, where the acquisition of wealth becomes a sign of admirable industry, piety, and even divine favor. We have witnessed, in brief, a dramatic rethinking of the function, worth, and fruits of work in Western culture. Without this theologically inspired reappraisal, capitalism and the free market system as we know them might never have developed. The world of work we know today, in other words, might be profoundly different. Among the lasting legacies of the Protestant Reformation are an understanding of work as a necessary, worthwhile, and ennobling enterprise; a view of work as constitutive of divine creativity and providence and, therefore, of what it means to be human; and a conviction that work is essential to Christian identity and community. Clearly, among the things that Luther, Calvin, and their fellow Reformers "re-formed" was the prevailing notion of work in the West. For those of us who desire to understand our own work or the larger world of work in the light of Christian tradition, this profound and thoroughgoing re-formation demands our attention.

Capitalism and Christianity: The Social Gospel

Fast-forward a few hundred years, and we find ourselves at another turning point for Christian notions of work: the Social Gospel movement of the late nineteenth and early twentieth centuries. This movement, which had a powerful and enduring effect on the shape of modern and contemporary Christianity, was inspired in large part by the plight of workers in an industrializing American society. The harsh realities of worker exploitation spawned a new lens for viewing Christian belief and practice—a lens that had a profound impact not only on the content and focus of modern Christianity but also on American understandings of civic virtue and the common good.

In the wake of the Civil War, old forms of mercantile capitalism began to disintegrate. In the "old" world, most capital was owned by farmers and small-business or cottage industry owners, the craft model of work was the norm, and most Americans lived and worked in rural settings. America's ministers were by and large Protestants who enthusiastically embraced laissez-faire capitalism. After the Civil War, however, this picture changed dramatically. With industrialization came mass migrations to American cities, where factory work became the norm and soon gave way to widespread poverty and human misery. Basic workplace safety and workers' rights programs of the kinds we take for granted today did not exist. Worker exploitation and discontent were rampant and led to frequent strikes.

The Social Gospel was the application of the good news of Christianity to this emerging world of industrialization and rapidly expanding capitalism. It asked the question, What does Christianity have to say to the embattled working class and, by extension, to the captains of industry and owners of capital whose fortunes are built on the backs of the struggling masses?

The movement's main innovation was the recognition that the gospel is relevant not merely to individual lives but to *social* realities as well. Poverty and unemployment are not simply economic or social challenges; they are theological ones as well. Building on the Second Great Awakening's emphasis on social reform as seen in the temperance and abolition movements, Social Gospelers took aim at the social challenges of their own day. They pointed out that biblical accounts do not depict Jesus' ministry as narrowly focused on individual persons nor even on the spiritual realm alone. Rather, Jesus is depicted as keenly aware of the ways in which individuals are embedded in social systems, groups, and hierarchies. His message focuses not only on individual persons but also on social groups such as "the poor." Moreover, the spiritual rebirth of persons that Jesus announces and makes possible depends upon the transformation of the social structures that form and sustain those persons. According to the Social Gospel, individual renewal and social transformation are two sides of the same coin. According to one leader of the movement, "Whatever the order of logic may be, there can be no difference in time between the two kinds of work; that we are to labor as constantly and as diligently for the improvement of the social order as for the conversion of man."[13] Jesus announced not only the salvation of the individual person but

> "We are to labor as constantly and as diligently for the improvement of the social order as for the conversion of man."

also the establishment of a world of plenty and peace—that is, *social* salvation.

Washington Gladden and Applied Christianity. This good news of a world of abundance in which diverse persons, creatures, and nations flourish in harmony with each other was a far cry from the often dirty, unsafe, and dehumanizing world of the nineteenth-century working class. Into this clash of realities stepped Washington Gladden, a congregational minister who is recognized today as the founder of the Social Gospel, although he described his religion as simply "applied Christianity." Gladden did not set out to change the face of American Protestantism, but in 1875, he found himself a young pastor in Springfield, Massachusetts, where shoe factory workers were protesting the lack of workplace protection, disability insurance, and the right to unionize. Gladden met with the striking workers and was moved to sympathize with their situation, even though the very people who owned and managed the shoe factories were members of his church. The following year, he put his support for workers' rights and his worries about the emerging shape of industrialism into print in *Working People and their Employers* (1876).[14] Here and elsewhere, Gladden brought Christian insights and theological categories to bear on the harsh realities of an industrializing nation. In the process, he called the church to account. He argued that the church was in need of conversion to authentic Christianity—to the movement inaugurated by Jesus in explicit sympathy with "the poor" and, by extension, its modern-day, working-class counterpart: "The one injurious and fatal fact of our present church work," said Gladden, "is the barrier between the churches and the poorest classes. The first thing for us to do is to demolish this barrier. . . . We are bound to address ourselves, at once and with all diligence, to the business of convincing the poor people that they are wanted, and will be made welcome in the churches."[15]

To make the poor genuinely welcome, Gladden came to realize, meant the church and its leaders could no longer align themselves with the ruling class. The time had come to acknowledge that capitalism had developed into a highly problematic system because its "natural" outcome was, on the one hand, an empowered and enriched class of owners or managers and, on the other hand, a disempowered class of workers who did not own the terms or products of their own labor. This was clearly *not* the realm of prosperity and peace announced by Jesus. Neither, however, was socialism the answer, Gladden insisted.

Instead of the selfishness and greed the prevailing system encouraged and rewarded, Gladden advocated cooperation, community, and profit sharing. He acknowledged that the wage system of labor was an important improvement over slavery, but it was still a far cry from humaneness. Rather than socialism, whose bureaucracy too often thwarted vital freedoms and squashed individual creativity, Gladden hoped for a reformed capitalism at whose center were profit-sharing enterprises in which workers had a real and lasting stake. He argued for "the Christianization of the present order," rather than its destruction.[16] Assuming that owners and managers were just as moral as anyone else, Gladden appealed to their goodwill and sense of justice, arguing that concern for the well-being of workers could go hand in hand with profitable business practices. Joining *with* workers to create genuinely cooperative enterprises would be a win-win situation for the capitalist class, he thought, and it would constitute a viable alternative to both a greed-infested capitalist system and a bureaucratic socialist state. Despite bitter disappointments, Gladden remained an idealist to the end, doggedly believing that capitalist America could make strides toward social improvement and spiritual perfection.

Despite the efforts of Gladden and his ilk, the plight of working Americans did not generate widespread support in the late 1800s. Some embraced what eventually came to be known as Social Darwinism—the idea that those who did not succeed in the new industrial world were simply unfit for the rigors of a capitalist future and, hence, should be allowed to fail so the rest of society could enter a new era of strength and prosperity. Others were so focused on their own survival that they felt they could not engage in system-wide analysis or protest. Still others saw the misery of the masses as the unfortunate but necessary growing pains of a society in transition. By contrast, those who embraced the Social Gospel experienced the social evils around them as rallying cries for change, clear indications that the time had come to speak out boldly on behalf of the kingdom of God.

Walter Rauschenbusch and Christian Socialism. The most famous of these Social Gospel prophets was Walter Rauschenbusch, a German-American congregational minister with a church in the Hell's Kitchen section of New York City. Here, amidst the suffering of a largely poor, immigrant population, Rauschenbusch felt the call of the Social Gospel. To his mind, no other version of Christianity could account for the world-diminishing evils of poverty and workplace injustice, nor offer the genuinely good news of salvation to such a context.

Early in his life as a pastor, Rauschenbusch preached that Christianity had a dual aim. For the individual, the goal was eternal life, while for humanity as a whole, it was the kingdom of God. Now, however, he came to appreciate that the kingdom of God had been Jesus' primary focus and was, hence, the proper aim of Christian mission and community. As Jesus himself made clear, his purpose was to usher in the reign of God—a world in which the peace, prosperity, and justice that God intends are fully actualized. The church's chief concern, said Rauschenbusch, should be the transformation of the world into the kingdom of God. To focus only or even primarily on the salvation of individual souls is to miss the bigger picture of the gospel, which is the transformation of society into the place of peace and justice God intends it to be. Salvation from sin in this context means not only the forgiveness of individual sins (e.g., adultery, theft, and hardness of heart) but also the amelioration of social sins such as predatory competition and greed, which result in any number of social injustices and devastate untold communities and lives.

The fact that these latter sins are embedded in systems and institutions led Social Gospelers to argue that their undoing requires the transformation of those very systems and institutions. Because deformations of work and workers were at the forefront of human misery in his day, Rauschenbusch took aim at the system that appeared to produce those deformations: capitalism. With the daily brutalities of working-class existence in mind, he argued that capitalism's systematic privileging of work's ownership and managerial classes over the working class, its cultivation of predatory competition, and its permissiveness toward power monopolies made it inimical to God's kingdom. Instead of a system premised on selfishness, competition, and greed, Rauschenbusch argued for a new way of organizing and valuing work that would emphasize cooperation and mutual caring. The church, he said, should lead the way toward Christian socialism, a system in which love of God and neighbor puts the brakes on the basest human instincts while inspiring cooperative enterprises that create both economic and social goods. Only a system whose highest aim is the common good instead of private gain should garner Christian support. "If money dominates," said Rauschenbusch, "the ideal cannot dominate. If we serve mammon, we cannot serve Christ."[17]

While Gladden held out hope for a reformed capitalism, Rauschenbusch's idealism was of a different sort. He was powerfully aware of human sin—the grasping for advantage and power that are hallmarks of human experience. Precisely because of this awareness, and because capitalism unabashedly invites and rewards this grasping, Rauschen-busch determined that capitalism is at odds with God's king-dom and must be opposed. For the vast majority of people, capitalism reduces work to a mere survival strategy. "The lowest motives for work are the desire for wages and the fear of losing them," he asserted. "Yet these are almost the only motives to which our system appeals."[18] The long-term out-come of such a degraded work experience is a lack of inter-est in and energy for one's work. While for employers this means a loss of productivity and profit, for workers the toll is even greater, insists Rauschenbusch: "A man's work is not only the price he pays for the right to fill his stomach. In his work he expresses himself. It is the output of his creative energy and his main contri-bution to the common life of mankind."[19] Both individual and community are diminished when meaningful work is the province of only a privileged few.

> "A man's work is not only the price he pays for the right to fill his stomach. In his work he expresses himself. It is the output of his creative energy and his main contribution to the common life of mankind."

A system in which most workers are deprived of a genu-ine ownership stake because they neither own the tools and materials of their work nor share in the profits produced by their efforts is a system that drives a wedge between the ownership and working classes, ensuring continued enmity and injustice. In this context, worker strikes and union-ization campaigns should come as no surprise, Rauschen-busch admonishes. They are a predictable response to a wage system of labor, a natural and even proper reaction to the degradation of what should be a life-giving dimen-sion of human experience. "Christ spoke of the difference between the hireling shepherd who flees and the owner who loves the sheep. Our system," argues Rauschenbusch, "has made the immense majority of industrial workers mere hirelings" who work out of fear and insecurity instead of "free minds who put love into their work because it is their own."[20] The economic losses borne by such an arrangement are staggering, Rauschenbusch admits, but "the moral loss is vastly more threatening." From the disintegration of workers' self-respect and physical health to the reduction in "human fellowship and kindliness," capitalism's ills are acute and chronic. Even when the cause of injury to workers lies clearly at industry's door, there is intense resistance to workplace reform. "It is dividends against human lives," reflects Rauschenbusch. Moreover, the competitiveness that capitalism breeds "exalts selfishness to the dignity of a moral principle."[21]

Considered theologically, concludes Rauschenbusch, capitalism is a major cause of social sin. The problem is not industry or commerce themselves but rather the way they are organized, which brings out the very worst in human beings. Indeed, he provokes, "If it were proposed to invent some social system in which covetousness would be deliberately fostered and intensified in human nature, what system could be devised which would excel our own for this purpose?"[22] America and much of the West may have staked their identity and fortunes on capitalism, but Rauschenbusch admonishes that "our national optimism and conceit ought not to blind us longer to the fact. Single cases of unhappiness are inevitable in our frail human life; but when there are millions of them, all running along well-defined grooves, reducible to certain laws, then this misery is not an individual, but a social matter, due to causes in the structure of our society and curable only by social reconstruction."[23]

At its heart, this reconstruction would need to involve a shift away from competition and hierarchy and toward cooperation and equality. Gladden's stubborn optimism notwithstanding, Rauschenbusch was resolute that capitalism—a system predicated on self-interest and competition—could not bear such a shift. As the failed efforts of Gladden and his peers demonstrated, "individual sympathy and understanding" were simply inadequate to achieve the deep structural changes necessary for social equality and justice.[24] While socialism was undeniably an imperfect alternative, its goal was at least the public good rather than narrower private ones. Rauschenbusch argued that if significantly tempered by Christianity's natural regard for freedom and creativity, socialism's tendency to sacrifice individual freedoms for the sake of the state could be contained. Ideally, democratic (or Christian) socialism would champion the common good while protecting the rights and dignity of the individual. With cooperation as both method and goal, the rigid barriers between owners and workers would dissolve, and the democratic impulse at the heart of American identity would quicken not simply the political terrain but economics as well. In that day, work would be not merely a means of survival but an avenue toward self-actualization, social justice, and communal flourishing; in other words, work would be both seed and fruit of the kingdom of God.

History has tended to paint Rauschenbusch and the Social Gospel movement with a positivist's brush—highlighting the hope for social transformation at the expense of the thoroughgoing realism about the depth and breadth of human evil.[25] Certainly, there was reason for optimism during Rauschenbusch's lifetime. In 1907 and 1908, for example, almost all the mainline Protestant churches in the United States adopted what was known as "The Social Creed"—a manifesto calling for work-focused reforms such as the elimination of child labor, the creation of disability insurance for injured workers, and the elimination of work on Sundays. Such prophetic consensus had the feel of real progress, and as we know, each of these reforms did eventually come to pass. In the words of one eminent historian of the period, "A third Great Awakening was occurring in American life, one that recovered the social spirit and kingdom goal of

Jesus."[26] However, to make much of Rauschenbusch's hope for social progress and perfection without at the same time emphasizing his sober awareness of the formidable obstacles posed by human frailty and social sin is to misconstrue the evidence and misrepresent the man and the movement. As Rauschenbusch himself acknowledged, "We shall never have a perfect social life, yet we must seek it with faith. At best there is always an approximation to a perfect social order. The kingdom of God is always but coming. But every approximation to it is worthwhile."[27]

> "We shall never have a perfect social life, yet we must seek it with faith."

For Social Gospel Christians like Rauschenbusch and Gladden, the re-formation of work along lines of shared enterprise and economic democracy was an indispensable feature of a kingdom-inspired society. Whether this re-formation entailed a Christian version of socialism or a retooled capitalism is less important for our purposes than the realization that in this distinctive moment of Christian history (the Social Gospel moment at the turn of the twentieth century), a strong consensus about working emerged. This consensus involved a positive valuation of both work and workers. Standing on the shoulders of Luther, Calvin, and their ilk, Social Gospel Christians embraced work as a crucial means of personal and social responsibility and, moreover, as an expression of religious fidelity and vitality. Reaching beyond these earlier Reformers, and in retrospect indicting the narrowness of their vision, Social Gospelers lifted up poor and working-class people as creatures of God, formed in the divine image and therefore worthy of respect and care. Insofar as capitalism systematically undermined such regard through a system of wage labor and class hierarchy, it warranted Christian concern and even protest.

If work was to achieve its potential as a reflection of divine creativity and providence and a means of human amelioration, then the status quo would not do. A more humane way of organizing work and workers was an absolute necessity, and the key was democracy, which Rauschenbusch described as "the expression and method of the Christian spirit."[28] Democracy was already the hallmark of American politics, and it was time to extend it to the economic system. Where capitalism tended to bring out the worst in people— greed, envy, and unrestrained acquisitiveness, democracy tempered human vices by promoting equality and freedom and checking the power of the privileged. What Rauschenbusch and his fellow Social Gospelers envisioned was a market system guided by democratic values and practices. Such a system would endow workers with the same kinds of freedoms, rights, and responsibilities as citizens of a democracy enjoy, and it would give them a real stake in the means and outcomes of production. Rather than a source of misery and degradation, work would be a humanizing endeavor—at once survival strategy, opportunity for self-expression and cooperation with others, and a vital form of service to the public good. Work, in other words, would help transform society toward peace and justice. It would, in effect, help usher in the reign of God.

Catholic Social Teachings

When Gladden, Rauschenbusch, and their peers began to articulate a social interpretation of Christianity, the United States was by and large a Protestant nation. By the time Rauschenbusch and Gladden died in 1918, Catholicism had become the largest religious denomination in the land. Size did not immediately translate into influence, however, for Catholics in nineteenth- and early-twentieth-century America were immigrants and mostly poor. Despite the triumphantly Protestant flavor of much Social Gospel rhetoric, the working class it championed was increasingly Catholic. For their own part, Catholic women and men mobilized impressively and with lasting results to combat the widespread poverty and hardship of those early immigrant generations. They founded countless schools, hospitals, and homes for destitute women and children. Before long, Catholics were famous for their social charity.[29]

However, as the nation industrialized and inequalities of wealth and power intensified, a gradual shift began to take place—a shift away from charity, with its focus on the needs of the individual, and toward justice, with its focus on the social and economic conditions that shape the individual's experiences and options. The catalyst for this transition from charity to justice in Catholic thought was the labor movement of the late nineteenth century, which was populated and often led by Catholic immigrants. With Pope Leo XIII's 1891 encyclical, *Rerum Novarum* (subtitled "On the Conditions of Labor"), the movement received encouragement from the very top, and the Catholic social movement was born.

In *Rerum Novarum,* Leo XIII took explicit aim at worker exploitation and the excesses of capitalism, arguing forcefully for a living wage, the necessity of labor unions to advocate for worker safety and rights, the importance of collective bargaining, and the fundamental dignity of workers. At the same time, he encouraged harmonious relations between rich and poor, owner and worker; eschewed violent protests; identified private property as a fundamental good; and affirmed, in clear opposition to socialism, that although markets should not be immoral, neither should they be overdetermined by the state. Perhaps the most important outcome of this historic encyclical was its identification of work as a moral category— an activity essential to human development. Work's primary purpose, it contends, is not to serve capitalism but to advance human flourishing.

Almost a century later, another papal encyclical would deepen Leo XIII's economic analysis while extending his insights into work and workers. In *Laborem Exercens* (On Human Work, 1981), Pope John Paul II affirms the conviction of *Rerum Novarum* and Vatican II documents that work is a vital dimension of human experience and community, part of what is meant by the biblical claim that humans are created in the divine image: "Man ought to imitate God, his creator, in working, because man alone has the unique characteristic of likeness to God."[30] Humans are called by God to work, John Paul II avers. Indeed, work distinguishes humans from other animals, making our interactions with the world uniquely intentional and creative. Work is not only a human duty, but "it maintains and develops our humanity," giving us a critical means of self-expression, learning, and caring for our families, as well as a way to serve the wider communities to which we belong. Work is not primarily a means to an economic end, insists John Paul II; rather, work has "an ethical value of its own" that is rooted in the fact that "the one who carries it out is a person, a conscious and free subject."

Thus, work's true value does not depend on wages, outcomes, or profits. Instead, work is valuable because of the worker—because the worker is a person, and all persons are created and loved equally by God: "Work is in the first place 'for the worker' and not the worker 'for work.'"[31] Instead of labor serving capital, which was capitalism's norm, capital should serve labor. The integrity of work and workers should be the driving force in the economy.

> "Work is in the first place 'for the worker' and not the worker 'for work.'"

If work's primary aim is humanization instead of economic output or gain, then we have a new moral plumb line for evaluating work practices and systems. The abiding question is this: Does work promote or thwart human flourishing? *Laborem Exercens* can be read as a meditation on this question. "All work," asserts John Paul II, "should be judged by the measure of dignity given to the person who carries it out." Work that helps the worker "realize his [or her] humanity" is good work. Work that allows one "to fulfill the calling to be a person" is good work.[32] In this analysis, it is not the *kind* of work that matters but its quality. Put differently, it is not the content of the work that is important but its impact on the worker's humanity.

Because of work's humanizing function, Catholic social teaching declares, work is a fundamental right of human beings. Work is a vital avenue to self-discovery and self-realization, offers a primary means of caring for one's family, and is necessary to the health of communities. Work is also, as noted earlier in this chapter, a way in which humans can participate in the life of God, contributing through our industry to the unfolding of the divine plan for the universe. For all these reasons, work is a basic human right. This means that unemployment is a travesty, a tragic loss of opportunity. "Unemployment, either in general or in certain sectors, is the opposite of a just and right situation," writes John Paul II. We should, then, strive to create a full-employment society so that all who are capable of working can do so. When necessary, the state should provide employment, although "it should not be unduly centralized." In the absence of good work for all citizens, the provision of unemployment benefits is necessary. This obligation stems from "the right to life and subsistence" that all people can claim.[33]

> "Unemployment, either in general or in certain sectors, is the opposite of a just and right situation."

Not only do all people have a right to work, but according to Catholic social teaching, they have a right to dignity-preserving work. This is work that includes fair pay, safe working conditions, disability and retirement insurance, reasonable work schedules, and time for rest and rejuvenation, so that one can provide for the needs of oneself and one's family over the long haul. A fair wage is one that allows the worker to enjoy the fruits of society's labor or, in John Paul

II's words, to have "access to those goods which are intended for common use: both the goods of nature and manufactured goods."[34] When wages are so low that workers cannot afford to live without shame in the larger society, or when they or their family members must go without proper nutrition or adequate shelter, clothing, or health care, then the wage system is unjust and should be changed. In relation to this kind of challenge, Catholic social teaching is clear that workers should be free to organize themselves in order to secure and safeguard their rights.

Dignity-preserving work is work that includes meaningful freedom, creativity, and responsibility for the worker. In *Laborem Exercens*, John Paul II declares that workers desire not only fair pay but also a share in the responsibility and creativity of the work process itself. Workers want input into how they work and how the fruits of their labor are used. The worker, says John Paul II, wants "to be able to know that in his work, even on something that is owned in common, he is working 'for himself.'" Capitalism's error, he writes, is that it turns workers into commodities, treating them like parts of a machine that can simply be replaced as needed instead of like the thinking, feeling, autonomous persons they actually are. Socialism is no better, he acknowledges, since it tends to reduce workers to cogs in a machine moved from above. In either case, workers become objects instead of subjects, tools of production rather than full-bodied persons.

According to *Laborem Exercens,* one answer to the problem of dignity-preserving work is democratic socialism or economic democracy. If the economy is to serve the worker, and not vice versa, then only an economic system that genuinely contributes to the positive development of workers can claim moral credibility. Only when workers have the freedom and authority to help determine working conditions, production methods and goals, and remuneration practices will they grow as both workers *and* human persons. In other words, only when workers are also owners can work achieve its humanizing potential. Thus, acknowledges John Paul II, exponents of Catholic social teachings over the years have made numerous proposals for shared ownership and cooperative management, for systems in which the risks and rewards of work are shared instead of being the sole possession of the ownership class. These proposals have consistently affirmed the importance and even sacred value of private property—thus avoiding any slippage into state socialism—but they have also emphasized (contra capitalism as it has been practiced thus far) that the right to property or ownership is not absolute. As John Paul II states in *Laborem Exercens*, Christian tradition "has always understood this right within the broader context of the right common to all to use the goods of the whole of creation: The right to private property is subordinated to the right to common use, to the fact that goods are meant for everyone." If private ownership of business does not produce access for everyone to the goods of creation, then such ownership is morally illegitimate.

Although Catholic social teachings and Protestantism's Social Gospel movement represent different ends of the American ecclesial spectrum, the fact remains that when it comes to the meaning of work and the treatment of workers, a clear and strong consensus exists. Both traditions articulate grave concerns about the dehumanizing tendencies of capitalism, and both view the extension of democracy into the economic realm as the most relevant and humane response to these tendencies. Both traditions have also struggled to maintain their viability and relevance over time. Catholic social teaching has been more successful in this respect, thanks to the centralized nature of the global church. Even here, however, the proliferation of publications, teachings, and conferences in support of economic justice and the transformation of work have had only a modest impact on the Catholic masses. Either the word is not getting out, or it is falling on deaf ears.

What messages about working *should* Christians in the pews hear these days? In chapter 1, we considered some of the defining characteristics of working in today's complex, globalized world. Next, we paused in chapter 2 to reflect on biblical insights into working. From the opening lines of the Hebrew Scriptures to the New Testament figures of Jesus, Paul, and James, we encountered a diverse set of reflections on the realities and challenges of work and workers that offered a surprisingly positive valuation of work and workers. In chapter 3, we have taken up the work-thinking of three distinctive moments in Christian history: the Protestant Reformation, the Social Gospel, and Catholic social teachings. The task that now remains is to ask what chapters 2 and 3 have to do with chapter 1. That is, what words of wisdom or critique does Christian theology offer to today's world of work? Conversely, how do contemporary work practices "talk back" to Christian tradition, challenging it to make revisions, embrace a broader perspective, or speak with greater precision or courage? What, finally, do twenty-first-century Christians need to have on their hearts and minds when it comes to working? On, then, to chapter 4.

4

toward a sacramental theology of work

In the course I teach on the meaning of work, students and I consider insights into working from numerous academic disciplines. We listen to voices from philosophy, sociology, religious studies, political theory, economics, and management, among others, with each discipline employing its own mix of methods and aims. In this book, we are interested in developing a *Christian* view of working—an understanding that takes seriously the insights, questions, and categories of Christianity's sacred texts and rich traditions. Chapter 2 lifted up key biblical texts for consideration, and chapter 3 did the same with several formative strands of Christian tradition. Our task in this chapter is to ask, So what? What difference does it make when the complex realities of working in today's world are considered through the lens of Christian scripture and tradition?

Let us begin with the end. To appreciate what is distinctive about a Christian interpretation, we need an understanding of the aim or end (*telos*) of human work proposed by the tradition. What, according to Christianity, is the purpose of work? Toward what end do we, or should we, labor? Numerous answers are possible. This book's brief and partial overview of Christian insights into working has highlighted several answers already, and others are possible as well. One of my favorite ways of thinking about the Christian *telos* or aim of existence is "life abundant."[1] A foundational claim of Christian tradition is that God creates life and desires its flourishing. Jesus says, "I came that they may have life, and have it abundantly" (John 10:10). Life abundant is life in its fullest, richest, most satisfying

> "I came that they may have life, and have it abundantly."

incarnation, and it is available both now, in this life, and in the life to come. Life abundant is God's intention not only for some of creation, not only for a privileged few, but for all. Abundance, flourishing, plenitude for *all*—this is God's desire for creation. This is the purpose to which God beckons the universe. God offers this gift, and in the service of this aim, human work finds its proper meaning and fulfillment.

For many Christians, the biblical story of the Garden of Eden articulates both the promise and the challenge of life abundant. This narrative depicts the aim of divine creativity: a world of copious beauty, diversity, harmony, and right relation in which humans enjoy a treasured place. At the same time, it reminds us that because of our own misdirected desires and misguided choices, we are in exile from that world. We live at a distance, so to speak, from God. Even as we are aware, deep within, of the plenteous goodness that could be ours, we find ourselves incapable of reaching it on our own. The good news of the gospel is that we are not, in fact, on our own. God has reached out to us through Jesus—God-become-flesh—to welcome us, and all of creation, into the fullness of God's being. The incarnation is God's extraordinary effort to draw us into life abundant, into God's reign of peace, justice, and plenitude. The incarnation is a gift of astounding creativity and worth, yet it is offered freely and with no expectation of return. Jesus offers his own life—his wisdom, courage, compassion, and wit; his spirit and his flesh; all of himself—as a gift, a love letter, a concrete expression of God's vital presence and deepest mercy, poured out for all.

When we open our hearts to this extraordinary gift, this wondrous work, we enter into that vital presence. We find ourselves enfolded by that deepest mercy. Our life *in* God's life—this, we realize, is life abundant, joy upon joy. Resting here is impossible, however, at least in this life. It is as if we have inhaled deeply, being filled with the life-giving breath of God. And now it is time to exhale, to allow that breath, that life-giving Spirit, to flow outward into the world around us. It seems that life abundant cannot be contained. It is for sharing.

Our breath is not really *ours*. We can lay no claim of ownership to the air we inhale. Nor can we say we deserve or have earned the air we breathe. It is simply there for us—a gift. So it is with work. God the worker creates and sustains the world. Formed in God's image, we, too, are workers, creators. But our work is derivative, dependent upon God's labor. Just as our breath is both ours and not ours—intimately interior, yet gone in a flash to inspire some other life—so is our work only "ours" for a moment. Even in that moment, the parable of the vineyard reminds us, our work is a gift. We do not "own" our work any more than we own a breath of air. Each is a life-sustaining gift, and the natural dynamism of each presses outward into the world. We are, in a sense, stewards of our work, temporary caretakers.

We might think of human work as a kind of sacrament: an outward and visible sign of an inward and invisible grace. In Christian tradition, a sacrament is an everyday, mundane substance—water, bread, wine—in which God's presence is experienced as palpably real. In the Eucharist, bread and wine are gifts from God. They are life and love poured out for us. But they are also the fruits of *our* labor: grain turned into bread, grapes pressed into wine.[2] Here, communion is the union of heaven and earth, spirit and flesh, divine work and human work. Together, they transform. To speak of work as cocreation is not to deny that God's work comes first and makes our work possible. Rightfully understood, human work responds to the divine work, in gratitude, in faithful imitation and creative extension. Through work, we attempt to share the good news of life abundant with all, especially those for whom abundance seems a distant or impossible goal. We offer our work to the world not because we are obligated to do so or because we have a debt to pay or an exchange to complete. We offer it because that is what work is—an offering, a gift, a sacrament.

With the ultimate aim of abundant life in sight, we can focus afresh on the shape of work in today's world. As Christians, we unapologetically use this aim as a lens through which to view and evaluate other aims and systems of the world. As Kathryn Tanner suggests in *Economy of Grace*, Christian theology should not understand itself as a minor discourse at the margins of economics. The Christian story is not only tangentially or occasionally related to economics. It *is* economics: "The whole Christian story, from top to bottom," insists Tanner, "can be viewed as an account of the production of value and the distribution of goods."[3] As creator of the world, God is the source of all things, all goods, and in God's household or economy, goods are made available to all who need them. No one has to compete for, earn, or deserve the goods of creation. They are, quite simply, freely given for the benefit of all. Just as our very life is bestowed upon us—a blessing we did not ask or compete for, so are all the goods of creation offered by God freely for the benefit of all.

The aim and effect of God's economy of grace is life abundant: plenty for all, and no one in need; the world's goods distributed so that all benefit from them. This account of the production and distribution of goods, this theological economy, argues Tanner, is the basis from which Christians can

> "The whole Christian story, from top to bottom, can be viewed as an account of the production of value and the distribution of goods."

and should evaluate the relative adequacy of other economies, other proposals and practices for the production and
distribution of goods. When we look at global capitalism,
then, we are not looking at *the* economy—the one and only
way things have always been or always will be. Rather, we see
an economy with its own distinctive story, aims, and vision
of the good life; an econ-
omy that has gone through
numerous transitions in
the past and will continue
to undergo change in the
future; an economy that can
be contested, questioned,
and altered; an economy that can be infiltrated and changed
from within by those whose hearts and lives have already
been transformed by a very different economy.

> **The aim and effect of God's economy of grace is life abundant: plenty for all, and no one in need.**

In an economy of grace, one of the goods offered freely
and for the benefit of all is work. God is a worker, Christian
tradition affirms, and the aim of God's work is life abundant.
Life abundant, mutual flourishing, the kingdom or reign of
God, the beloved community—the particular language Christians use to articulate the purpose of work is less important
than the core conviction, indeed, the saving experience, that
God's work gives life and bestows goods on all who need them.
Our work is a gift. Through
it, we can imitate and participate in God's work.

Divine and human work
may ultimately take aim
at life abundant, but what
does that look like in real
life? How does that *telos*
square with the often harsh realities of work we encountered
in chapter 1 of this book? One way of thinking about work
that might help Christians interface with contemporary work
realities is a simple, threefold typology: work understood as

> **In an economy of grace, one of the goods offered freely and for the benefit of all is work.**

subsistence, selfhood, and service. This typology brings the challenges posed by today's work practices into focus even as it allows us to see how the Christian hope of life abundant has transformative implications for human work.

Work as Subsistence

Christian scriptures and tradition do not, on the whole, romanticize work. Jesus and his comrades were working-class people well attuned to the struggles and joys of subsistence living. Paul told his comrades that if they wanted to eat, they would have to work, and he emphasized the importance and dignity of manual labor. Martin Luther argued that the everyday labors of ordinary people can be a service to God more valuable than a priest's. Social Gospelers and proponents of Catholic social teachings broadened the scope of Christian doctrine to promote the full humanity of working-class men, women, and children.

Contemporary Christians who consider the weight of their tradition will conclude that subsistence is a proper fundamental aim of human work. Taken seriously, this claim means Christians have a moral obligation to strive for a world in which work is available to all who are able and in which work enables minimal standards of living. Because work creates livelihood, it is to be acknowledged and advanced as a kind of prerequisite to basic human existence. In an economy of grace, work is a public good, not a private one. It is meant for all, not only for those who compete successfully to attain it or for those who have the right connections or a lucky birthright. Economies that are premised on some "acceptable" level of unemployment are, by this standard, morally unacceptable. If, in a capitalist economy, the private sector cannot produce enough jobs to go around, then government can close the gap, providing jobs at just below market value so as not to undercut market forces. Christians who recognize subsistence as a fundamental aim of human work will work toward a full-employment society, beginning with their own churches and businesses.

What if the creation of good work were added to a church's outreach mission or a business's goal sheet? How might the organizational chart, the allocation of charitable dollars, or the choice of community partners change? What if job creation as an institutional goal were taken as seriously as objectives like increased efficiency, productivity, membership, or profit? Wouldn't more people with jobs mean more people joining the economy, buying goods and services, making charitable donations, and paying taxes? If we want a full-employment society, a society in which life—and hence livelihood—is available to all and not only to some, then these are the kinds of questions Christians need to be asking (and answering!).

Beyond being available to all, work has to pay. A full-time job should provide a livelihood—that is, sufficient resources for life's necessities: adequate food, shelter, clothing, education, and medical care. Adam Smith, father of capitalism, was explicit in saying workers' wages must be enough to provide the worker and the worker's family with the necessities for humane living.[4] In recent years, the distinction between a "minimum" wage and a "living" wage has been helpful in highlighting that although a minimum wage is purportedly the wage necessary to support basic but decent living, study upon study reveals that in many towns and cities, a forty-hour-per-week minimum-wage job does not, in fact, support such living. If a nation's or state's minimum wage is not, in reality, a living wage, then Christians are obligated to work for change.[5]

> Adam Smith, father of capitalism, was explicit in saying workers' wages must be enough to provide the worker and the worker's family with the necessities for humane living.

What is a living wage in *your* town or city? If you don't know, check out one of the living-wage calculators available online.[6] Better yet, use your own household's needs and expenses as a starting point for making your own calculation: consider your monthly or annual expenses, cut the frills, keep the basics, and then determine the hourly wage necessary to support that level of living. If the amount you arrive at is higher than minimum wage, then minimum wage should be higher. If the life that is possible on minimum wage is, in all honesty, a sorry excuse for a life, then there is important work to be done. If the lowest-paid workers in your church or workplace are making less than a living wage, then there is important work to be done. The good news is that there are plenty of others with whom to join forces in this work and more ways than ever to collaborate with them.

Subsistence is a vital ingredient in a Christian view of working. It is the foundation, the starting point, the indispensable first step. In its absence, life abundant is impossible. The gift of work is not only for some. It is a public good, for the benefit of all. One aim of our work as Christians, then, is to ensure that work as subsistence or livelihood is available to all.

Work as Selfhood

In the books, essays, interviews, and documentaries about work and workers I have studied in the past ten years, one of the most memorable snapshots of work is the one featuring Sam and his peer group of homeless recyclers in San Francisco (chapter 1). Without romanticizing the horrors of homelessness or ignoring the structural causes of homelessness, we may still find ourselves deeply moved by this portrait of human dignity against all odds. Clearly, there is something about work that cultivates selfhood, at least in a work-centered society like ours. When it provides daily structure, resources for survival, a place on the social map, and some degree of autonomy, even scavenging trash can be a source of self-respect.

In Christian tradition, the importance of work to personal identity or self-regard is robustly affirmed. Even God's personhood is at least partially constituted by work, as God is portrayed in scripture as a diligent, attentive, and profoundly imaginative worker. For the apostle Paul, we recall, work is an indispensable means of developing self-reliance, self-discipline, and an awareness of how one should relate to larger wholes. For John Calvin, it is a divinely ordained font of self-knowledge and self-direction. Work gives our lives purpose and stability, he insists, grounding our identity and centering our passions. According to the Social Gospel, work is a crucial opportunity for individual self-expression and self-actualization. It is, moreover, a cultivator of personal responsibility and the key to social progress. In Catholic social teachings, work conveys dignity on the individual, gives him or her access to the goods of creation, and is a primary avenue to human flourishing.

Throughout the generations, Christian tradition has affirmed work as an important means to human selfhood. God's intention for creation is not simply to have life but to have it *abundantly*. Insofar as human work is part of that realization, its purpose is not simply survival or livelihood, but self-actualization as well. Just as the work of creation is God's unique self-expression—an autonomous communication of God's being, industry, imagination, and benevolence—so should human work be. When it is not, Christians are obliged to protest and work for change. This is precisely what Rauschenbusch and his Social Gospel peers and Pope Leo XIII and his Catholic colleagues did in response to the widespread dehumanization and exploitation of workers in the heyday of American industrialization. For too many people, work offered neither subsistence nor selfhood. Because of its individualistic tenor, Christian doctrine was of limited relevance and assistance. This was a moment when the realities of work "talked back" to Christian tradition, challenging the church to reframe the good news for a new day. The reinterpretation of sin and salvation as *social* categories instead of only individual ones, and of the kingdom of God as a future *and* present reality, were major theological innovations that had far-reaching ecclesial, social, and political effects.

These innovations are now part of Christian tradition—precedents to which we can appeal as we attempt to understand and challenge deformations of human work. A notion of sin that targets not only the ways in which individuals turn away from or ignore God but also the ways in which systems, policies, institutions, and groups become obstacles to God's intentions for creation can help us identify and combat these deformations. As we saw in chapter 1, both new and old perversions of work as selfhood are alive and well in today's "new economy," and these perversions demand Christian response. Despite new technologies that have in many respects revolutionized contemporary work, many workers today still face perennial challenges like poverty wages, socially devalued work, workplace exploitation, the loss or chronic absence of work, and the curtailment of autonomy, individuality, and personal agency at work. The experience of any one of these can be destructive to a worker's self-worth. Too often, one negative work feature follows or exacerbates another. As Barbara Ehrenreich asks, "If you hump away at menial jobs 360-plus days a year, does some kind of repetitive injury of the spirit set in?"[7]

> "If you hump away at menial jobs 360-plus days a year, does some kind of repetitive injury of the spirit set in?"

Rather than functioning as an imitation and extension of God's life-giving, spirit-nurturing labor, human work can be a source of disfiguring trauma. Instead of enhancing the knowledge, skills, and self-worth of the laborer, work frequently tears the self down. Obvious examples would be the kind of exploitation that occurs in sweatshops or the sex trafficking industry, but less dramatic forms are no less damaging to the spirit, especially when they are prolonged. Spending years in a job that doesn't utilize or develop one's skills, or where one's opinion or contributions are routinely ignored, or where one's work doesn't produce anything of real quality or meaning, or where one has no hope of advancement—these kinds of daily diminutions of self add up.

Full Participation. It can be difficult for those of us who enjoy significant degrees of autonomy in our work to appreciate what it is like to have very little freedom or voice as workers, but this is another significant source of "spirit injury." Whether at a telemarketing firm that enforces a strict dress code even though employees never encounter customers face-to-face, or at an automotive plant that imposes new efficiency strategies without consulting workers, daily curtailments of human freedom and creativity take their toll, particularly when the intention is to reinforce power hierarchies rather than improve work or develop workers. Too many workers in today's economy have to check their creativity, autonomy, and pride at the door, entering a world where someone else's vision, authority, bank account, and selfhood rule. Despite predictions by post-Fordist theorists of increased worker freedom and fulfillment in the "new" economy, most workers today experience profound and prolonged powerlessness on the job. This experience takes a toll not only on one's self-worth but also on one's relationships with others, including coworkers. It also has much larger implications, provokes William Greider: "Where did

> "Where did citizens learn the resignation and cynicism that leads them to withdraw as active citizens? They learned it at the office; they learned it on the shop floor."

citizens learn the resignation and cynicism that leads them to withdraw as active citizens? They learned it at the office; they learned it on the shop floor. This real-life education in who has power and who doesn't creates a formidable barrier to ever establishing an authentic democracy in which [citizens] are genuinely represented and engaged."[8]

In response to the far-reaching and sobering implications of freedom-curtailing work, we might recall that Catholic social teachings and the Social Gospel lift up economic democracy as the best approximation of an economy of grace's production and distribution of goods. Economic democracy is the extension of democracy into the economic realm; it is basically a market system guided by democratic values and practices. With thoroughgoing intentionality, economic democracy cultivates work as both subsistence and selfhood. Such a system can take many forms, but it generally involves shared ownership and cooperative management. My students are always fascinated to learn that economic democracy is not just a theory or a pipe dream; it is, in fact, a reality in today's world in big and small ways.

The most celebrated example of economic democracy is Mondragón, a series of business cooperatives in the Basque region of northern Spain. Mondragón was begun almost fifty years ago by five men who were inspired and mentored by a Catholic priest named Don José María Arizmendiarrieta, and it continues to exemplify Catholic social teachings.[9] Today, Mondragón is a network of 150 for-profit cooperative enterprises in industries as diverse as real estate, education, and manufacturing, with some 60,000 employees and annual revenues of $8 billion. At the heart of Mondragón is the principle of the dignity of work and workers. That dignity is secured and promoted in myriad ways, chief among them shared ownership, democratic decision making, fair pay, and social justice.

Every Mondragón worker is also an owner. Each worker-owner shares in both the risks and the rewards, and each participates actively in all major policy decisions. To join a Mondragón cooperative, one must invest the equivalent of one year's salary. This means that all workers are investors with an ownership stake in the company. Those who cannot afford such an outlay may borrow the amount from the Mondragón bank and repay it over the course of three years. This practice provides access to meaningful work even to those without economic means.

Each Mondragón business is a democracy, with all major decisions of policy and practice requiring a majority vote in a one-person/one-vote system. Smaller decisions are made by councils whose representatives are elected by cooperative members. In this model, workers not only are *permitted* to have a voice in how work is defined, managed, and compensated, but are *expected* to do so. They are also encouraged to educate themselves and to develop leadership and problem-solving skills so they can make optimal contributions to the enterprise. Far from being a dehumanizing experience, work is an opportunity for growth, and not simply for higher-wage workers, but for everyone.

To ensure fair pay for all, Mondragón limits pay ratios between its top executives and field or factory workers. These ratios, which are voted on by all members of a cooperative, range from 3:1 to 9:1, with an average of 5:1. As a result, top executives make up to 30 percent less than their non-Mondragón counterparts, midlevel managers and professionals at Mondragón make competitive salaries, and the lowest-paid Mondragon employees make about 15 percent more than comparable non-Mondragón workers. Thus, the salary range at Mondragón is compressed relative to the traditional work world, with a significantly lower ceiling but a much higher basement. So that everyone receives a living wage, some are willing to compromise. Although Mondragón's highest-wage earners could earn substantially more money in other settings, they report that the satisfaction of genuinely meaningful work that contributes to the common good makes the monetary trade-off worth it. Interestingly, neighborhoods in Mondragón are not economically stratified. Workers of all ranks and salary levels live together. Economic democracy, it seems, is good for community.

It is also good for business. In fifty years, only one Mondragón company has failed. That compares with the typical failure rate for small-business start-ups of around 50 percent.[10] Mondragón workers rarely fail, either. Where the norm in a traditional capitalist economy is to eliminate workers (downsizing) during economic hard times, Mondragón businesses have adopted a no-layoff policy. If market forces require a scaling back or reconfiguration of a cooperative, displaced workers are relocated to other Mondragón cooperatives without sacrificing wages. If technological innovations render a worker's skill set obsolete, he or she is retrained and returned to the Mondragón workforce. With the ideal of full employment in mind, job creation is a top priority in the Mondragón cooperatives. This fact is demonstrated by worker-owners' election to reduce their profit margin in order to finance growth and, hence, create jobs. In a six-year period from 1995 to 2001, Mondragón cooperatives more than doubled their workforce. They also enjoyed steady growth in productivity and profits, and those profits were shared by all worker-owners.

Although Mondragón is the largest and best-known example of economic democracy in today's world, there are plenty of smaller, less-heralded examples, including many in the United States. Although the particularities of each enterprise may vary, sometimes considerably, what remains the same is that workers are also owners who share the risks, responsibilities, and rewards of their work. These features provide no guarantee of success in today's volatile market economy, but most worker-owned enterprises have thus far outperformed traditional capitalist firms while providing significantly higher-quality experiences for workers. Work as both subsistence and selfhood may be increasingly rare in today's advanced capitalist society, but it is apparently a natural fit for economic democracy. The fact that economic democracy can exist on a small scale alongside capitalist economies, with employee-owned enterprises competing successfully with traditional capitalist firms while offering workers significant value-added outcomes in the form of increased autonomy, dignity, and social justice, means that over time, demand for employee-owned enterprise could increase.

Christians interested in the dignity of work and workers will want to add their voices to the demand and, where possible, make their own forays into economic democracy. This would not mean leaving capitalism behind so much as transforming it from within. Over time, this transformation might lead to entirely new and more life-giving economic forms. If we can agree that meaningful work and a living wage—that is, both selfhood and subsistence—are goods to which all should have access, then employee ownership and economic democracy are viable pathways to those goods. For Christians who want human work to imitate and extend the dignity, creativity, autonomy, and plenitude of God's work, economic democracy is an idea whose time has come. Workers who are also owners become practiced in seeing that the bottom line is not the only aim worth pursuing and competition not the only route to prosperity. Good work, we learn, is work that is good for everyone. Life abundant is for all.

As always, the place to begin is close to home, with one's own work situation and one's own church or spiritual community. Economic democracy for a church sounds like an odd idea, since any talk of "ownership" seems theologically misguided. However, as the body of Christ whose mission is to embody Christ in the world, the church is arguably the most appropriate place for an economy of grace to be practiced and exemplified. Many denominations and congregations already embrace democratic forms of organization and leadership—electing councils, vestries, or elders by votes of the full membership and empowering those elected to set policy, guide spending, and determine compensation. Mirroring the start-up investment required by workers in most employee-owned enterprises, many churches also limit membership with voting rights to those who are investors in the church—that is, those who contribute their time, talent, and/or treasure. Most churches also strive for a version of full employment as they attempt to provide meaningful "jobs" or ministries for each and every person who desires to be involved in the work of the church. In most cases, these jobs have equal dignity and communal regard. It doesn't matter whether one sings in the choir, coordinates the annual stewardship campaign, helps maintain the playground, or volunteers regularly in a social justice ministry; every job is important to the life and mission of the church, and every worker is equally valued by the congregation. In these and other ways, the principles of economic democracy are already at work in the church.

There is, however, always room for a more full-bodied embrace of an economy of grace, so consideration should be given not only to the ways in which the work of church members is being organized, managed, and valued, but also to the work of church staff, especially lay staff. Are all staff members paid a living wage? Do they have a genuine voice in matters related to their work environment, job responsibilities, and performance evaluation? Are they profiting from the "success" of the church? Here, we might think of "profit" not only in monetary terms—ensuring, for example, that staff receive pay raises or benefits enhancements whenever possible—but also in terms of human development capital. Do we offer our lowest-paid staff members the resources of our church members—benefits like financial counseling, pro bono legal work, a weekend with their family at a church member's vacation home, or even help in developing new skills or relationships that would lead to a better job? In other words, are we trying to "grow" our church staff as intentionally and creatively as we do our church members? Are our lowest-paid employees explicitly included in our vision and practices of life abundant? Are we ensuring that the goods of creation (that is, all good things) are being distributed to all and not just to some?

Beyond the church, we should also consider how we might integrate the humanizing principles of economic democracy into our own work lives. No matter where on the organizational flow chart we find ourselves, we can look for opportunities to make work "work" for everyone. The same kinds of questions we asked about the intention and practices of the church should be asked of our own workplaces. Depending on where we stand in the organization, one question or another will make the most sense for us to target as a first step. The more institutional power we have, the more responsible we are for making our work, and the work our work makes possible, as humanizing and life-giving as it can possibly be. When we consider our role as consumers rather than workers, we can promote economic democracy by patronizing employee-owned companies. A simple Web search will uncover dozens of such companies, as well as organizations like the National Center for Employee Ownership, which provides information and technical support for those interested in exploring employee ownership. Few companies embody the concept as thoroughly and thoughtfully as the Mondragón cooperatives do, but every step toward worker dignity and participation is a step in the right direction.

In relation to our study of economic democracy, I sometimes ask my students to think about where in the grand work scheme they hope to be in five years, ten years, and twenty years. Then I challenge them to imagine how they might be able, within that work context, to bring the principles of economic democracy to bear on their work. I encourage readers of this book to try the same thought experiment, except instead of imagining your future work, think about your work right now: who makes decisions; whose opinions, experiences, and welfare are considered when decisions are made; who profits from whose work, and with whom those profits are shared; and how traditional economic values like efficiency, productivity, and profit relate to the values of an economy of grace, such as dignity, freedom, relationship, and indiscriminate benevolence and generosity. Then look for inroads to abundance—concrete ways to make those grace-filled values a reality in your specific work context. Ideally, those ways will not be singular or isolated gestures but habitual practices that bring you into meaningful relationships with others who may benefit from those practices, who find their own conscience awakened by your example, or who are eager to join your efforts. The possibilities for moving workplaces and work practices toward democratic models of participation and governance that promote the flourishing of all God's people are diverse and plentiful. The important thing is to get moving.

Practices of Inclusion. In addition to trying to promote humanizing work at institutional and systemic levels, personal-scale efforts also are vitally important. A small but significant everyday practice that tends to reinforce unhealthy relationships to work while exacerbating class differences is the ubiquitous conversation question, "So, what do you do?" For members of the professional and managerial classes, this question is generally a well-intended entrée to a new acquaintanceship, a seemingly harmless social ritual that occasionally gives way to deeper inquiry. Among this demographic, it is common for topics related to work to be the center of conversation at family gatherings and other social events. What one does for a living can be reasonably expected to shed genuine light on one's selfhood—one's interests, gifts, convictions, and tastes. Work, then, reveals and shores up selfhood. However, for the unemployed and working class, such questions and conversations can diminish self-esteem and create worries about one's social worth. (They can also unveil the work-centered hubris of the one posing the question!) Given the individual and social power of work in contemporary society and, at the same time, the dignity-diminishing effects of that power on some members of society, Christians might consider following the example of Barbara Brown Taylor, Episcopal priest and author. Realizing the class privilege involved in the "And what do you do?" social ritual, Taylor determined to stop asking the question. Instead, she developed the habit of asking questions about person rather than profession, self rather than status: "What feeds you? How do you spend your days?"[11]

Work may be a vital source of selfhood in today's culture, but its social importance can also hurt and divide. Thus, even as Christians advocate for work that supports human dignity and freedom, work that develops rather than diminishes selfhood, we want to be mindful of the many small and seemingly inconsequential ways we make too much of work and thereby offend or hurt those around us. It is so easy to equate selfhood with work and to forget that work is what we *do*, not who we *are*. Even when work is ideally self-actualizing and life-giving, even when it serves noble aims and accomplishes good things, it is not the aim of existence.

> Barbara Brown Taylor developed the habit of asking questions about person rather than profession, self rather than status: "What feeds you? How do you spend your days?"

As the Protestant Reformers so compellingly argued, work is a means, not an end.

For some of us, this truth can take a while to sink in. Those with work that is less than they would like—less meaningful, less lucrative, less important, less exciting—can become so convinced that work should be the fulfillment of all their needs and aspirations that their non-ideal work situation becomes a source of real and persistent negativity in their lives. Certainly, we want to wring as much meaning and satisfaction as possible from our work, and certainly there are times to protest work's injustices and indignities, but as the author of Ecclesiastes knew, work is only one part of life, and to place too much store in its fruits is to chase after wind.

The church has historically had a special role to play here by offering an alternative scale of value by which to measure one's worth and offer one's work. In the United States, we have seen this dynamic at play in especially powerful ways in African American communities. From slavery's "invisible institution" to today, the black church has been a vitally important crucible of human dignity, freedom, creativity, and leadership.[12] Benjamin Mays and Joseph Nicholson's classic description of the transformative effect of church on those whose work the world overlooks or despises is worth quoting in this respect:

> A truck driver of average or more than ordinary qualities becomes the chairman of the Deacon Board. A hotel man of some ability is the superintendent of the Sunday church school of a rather important church. A woman who would hardly be noticed, socially or otherwise, becomes a leading woman in the missionary society. A girl of little training and less opportunity for training gets the chance to become the leading soprano in the choir of a great church. These people receive little or no recognition on their daily job. There

is nothing to make them feel that they are "somebody." Frequently their souls are crushed and their personalities disregarded. . . . But in the church on X Street, *she* is Mrs. Johnson, the Church Clerk; and *he* is Mr. Jones, the Chairman of the Deacon Board.[13]

Sabbath Practices. Biblical tradition offers an important antidote to the overvaluing of work that occurs across the economic and social spectrum. Thanks to technological innovations of the past few decades, work in the new economy is in certain ways more generous and nonhierarchical than ever. In other respects, work is greedier than ever, erasing the boundaries between office and home, work and play. The same technologies that make collaboration, flextime, and flexspace more accessible to today's workers also bring work increasingly into the home and into every "nonwork" venue imaginable. The diffusion of work into every crevice of existence is especially characteristic of the professional, managerial, and ownership classes, where work's 24/7 availability deepens the identification of self with work. Where some of our fellow citizens are forced by low wages and unaffordable housing and health care to work two or more jobs, involuntarily saturating their lives with work, too many of us at the other end of the spectrum acquiesce to work's domination without a real fight. Among the professional class in America, overwork is nearing epidemic proportions. Consumerism is a major cause: to feed the shopping/buying habit we have to work longer hours. Other factors are at play as well, including a lack of imagination and resolve. Of particular relevance to religious

> "These people receive little or no recognition on their daily job. But in the church on X Street, *she* is Mrs. Johnson, the Church Clerk; and *he* is Mr. Jones, the Chairman of the Deacon Board."

people is the degree to which economic versions of meaning and value have all but eclipsed other fonts of meaning. Many of us work more than we need to because we believe, perhaps at some subconscious level, that the economic sphere is where meaning and selfhood reside. We may protest that we value family, community, and/or God more than work, but in many instances our actions belie our real priorities.

For those whose lives are diminished or disfigured by too much work, whether voluntary or not, the biblical tradition of Sabbath stands as an important salve.[14] In the creation narrative of Genesis 1 and 2, the Sabbath is God's consecration of rest, *menuha*, at the conclusion of six days of prolific work. We might notice that God's work in these days is characterized not only by wise technique and astounding productivity but also by moments of pause and reflection—time for taking stock of the work, appreciating its quality, and considering its overall worth. Despite the humane pace of daily work that God embraces, a special day of rest is still established. It is almost as if God realizes work's ability to overwhelm other priorities and saturate one's consciousness, so a holy and complete rest is blessed and consecrated. This rest is not only for some but for all. It is for God, for humans, and for animals. It is, as Exodus 20 makes explicit, not only for some workers but for all of them: Remember the sabbath day, and keep it holy. Six days you shall labor and do all your work. But the seventh day is a sabbath to the LORD your God; you shall not do any work—you, your son or your daughter, your male or female slave, your livestock, or the alien resident in your towns (Exod. 20:8-10).

In Jewish practice, the Sabbath is not only a day of rest, it is a day of rejuvenation—a day for dwelling with God, to be sure, but not necessarily by withdrawing from the rest of the world. When viewed through Sabbath eyes, what we see is not the world's instrumentality or profitability but its mystery, its profound holiness.[15] What was yesterday merely a raw material for manufacturing is today a singular jewel of creation. The worker we barely noticed a moment ago is now a beloved and irreplaceable child of God. Through Sabbath eyes, the world's tender beauty and the worker's fragile sanctity come into focus, expanding our vision of what matters and who counts. However, if these windows onto life abundant are to be anything more than fleeting glimpses, then our eyes must be trained, our hearts and minds habituated. In a consumer society where working and shopping take place around the clock and where our wants and desires are continually manipulated with ever-increasing sophistication, the recalibration of priorities and the refocusing of vision take time and commitment. Especially in this context, the Sabbath can function as a kind of manual reset button, a potent reminder of who we really are and what really matters. As Wayne Muller writes, "Sabbath creates a marker for ourselves so, if we are lost, we can find our way back to our center."[16]

> When viewed through Sabbath eyes, what we see is not the world's instrumentality or profitability but its mystery, its profound holiness.

> "Sabbath creates a marker for ourselves so, if we are lost, we can find our way back to our center."

Church can be an important Sabbath moment—a space apart, a time set aside, a community of support in which to re-member ourselves. In the liturgy, we are immersed in the pace and priorities of an economy of grace, where meaningful work abounds and both body and spirit are plentifully nourished. Sabbath can also come in different doses and on different days. A Sabbath practice can be anything that offers sacred rest, spiritual rejuvenation, or self-sustaining reorientation. It can be a daily time of meditation or centering prayer, a walk, an hour curled up with a good book, a meal lingered over with a dear one. Emerging from such sacred space and time, we can see the scarcities, exclusions, and humiliations of traditional economy for what they are: a failure of both imagination and will. And we can draw on new pools of resolve, energy, and solidarity as we try again to live into the wondrous plenty of God's amazing grace.

Sabbath rest, then, is not about sleep. It invites us not to close our eyes but to open them, not to roll over but to wake up! When through Sabbath practices we remove ourselves from the frenetic pace of our workaday lives, taking a step back from the rat race and the spirit-sapping pressure or petty humiliations of so much of work in today's world, then our hearts begin to heal, our passion for justice and mercy is rekindled, and our connections to God, neighbor, and all of creation are renewed.

Work as Service

Work in a Christian paradigm enables not only subsistence and selfhood but also service. As Martin Luther emphasized, serving others is *the* reason we work. God calls us to love and serve our neighbor, and it is through our work that we respond to that call. The opportunities for serving others with our work are multiplicitous and need not be rehearsed here, but we might pause for a brief moment to consider that Luther's point is not that Christians should serve others in our free time, but that the purpose of our *work* is to serve others. This means service is not something we are summoned to do on the side. Rather, it should be the center of our activity. Whatever our daily work, its primary purpose, insists Luther, is to serve others. No matter our specific work—teacher, lawyer, machinist, artist, janitor, physician, sales clerk, parent—the *purpose* of that work is to serve others. The service itself spawns meaning and joy, so that work as service is generative of work as selfhood.

We have already acknowledged that this perspective can function to perpetuate work inequalities and social injustice by reinforcing the status quo and discouraging efforts to contest one's position in life. However, if this idea of work as service is embraced in the context of or in the midst of efforts to embrace an economy of grace of the sort we have been considering in this chapter, then the life-giving and countercultural possibilities of work understood as service are underscored. What if, in resonance with an economy of grace's offer of life abundant, we took seriously Luther's mandate that work's purpose is to serve others? What if we took it seriously in our families, churches, and schools so that a main message our children and youth hear about work as they grow up is that its aim is service? From the standpoint of one who engages young people in that key transitional period between home and career, I suggest that such a message could make a huge difference. If our young people get consistently positive messages from these formative social institutions about the meaning of work, if they hear from people they respect—parents, teachers, coaches, and ministers—that the highest purpose of work is service to others, then they will have the crucial moral authority and emotional support they need to stand up to consumer-focused definitions of work's purpose. My experience is that today's young people *want* to pursue work as service, even if it means sacrificing certain levels of material achievement, because they understand that life

> Luther's point is not that Christians should serve others in our free time, but that the purpose of our *work* is to serve others.

is about meaning, not money, but they are under so much pressure from socially sanctioned, media-promoted, materialistic notions of success that it is difficult to resist those seductions.

It is precisely here that religion must enter, offering a robust alternative vision of purpose and success, as well as concrete practices and supports for embracing that vision. Work understood as a gift from God and a gift for others would be part of such an alternative vision. So, too, would work as a sacrament—an outward and visible sign of an inward and invisible grace. An economy of grace has to go toe-to-toe with an economy of competitive consumerism, offering a viable and compelling alternative for the sake of our children and grandchildren and, indeed, for the sake of all creation.

In this chapter, we have lifted up a vision of life abundant as the *telos* or aim of existence. We have said that the source of this abundance is the indiscriminately generous Divine whose work gives life to all things and desires their flourishing: not only life, but life abundant, and not only for some, but for all. As we are created in the divine image, our work as humans can and should imitate God's work, supporting the flourishing of others by distributing the blessings or goods of creation to all who need them. In an economy of grace, one of those goods is work itself. Work, we have seen, is the foundation of survival, a vital source of selfhood, and an important opportunity for service. Despite its centrality to human existence and flourishing, work in today's world is a good that is by no means available to all. Too many have no work at all, and even more have work whose goodness is in question: work that is not an adequate livelihood; work that destroys or diminishes dignity, creativity, or autonomy; work that fails to serve the real needs of others. In our day, work is largely defined by an economy that values competition, consumerism, and profit above all else and that depends upon a large, cheap, and disempowered working class, a small but miserable workless class, and a star-gazing professional class that would rather fawn over the owners than make common cause with the workers. If an economy of grace is to rival, displace, or transform the reigning economy, then Christians have got to get to work!

The Greatest Work/Gift

There are many, many ways to work on behalf of life abundant, several of which we have discussed in the pages of this chapter. There are also, as we have seen, myriad strong supports to be found in Christian tradition: sacred texts, inspiring movements, and wise insights into God's work and human work. One thing we have not considered adequately, and with which this book will conclude, is what difference the work of Christ makes for human working. The question of Christ's work is famously complicated and cannot be adequately explored in this context, but I will nevertheless attempt to offer in these final paragraphs a few suggestions for how the one whom Christians know as God's greatest work, God's greatest gift, can illuminate our understanding and practice of our own work.[17]

We Christians like to dwell on the uniqueness of Jesus. We emphasize that he was wiser, smarter, or braver than everyone else, or that he was more loving or faithful or self-giving than anyone else, or that he was the only one who ever has been or ever will be both fully human and fully divine. I am not interested here in disputing any of these claims. I do, however, want to suggest that these kinds of assertions can lead to such a heroic view of Jesus—such a high Christology, as theologians would say—that they obscure other truths about Jesus the Christ and the character of the work he undertook.

From the earliest centuries, Christian tradition has privileged heroic narratives of creation, redemption, and consummation at the expense, often, of other versions of reality. For instance, although the opening verses of Genesis narrate

God's primordial work as the creation of the universe out of "the deep" (Hebrew, *tehom*), the theologians of the early Christian church argued vehemently that God had created the universe *ex nihilo,* out of nothing.[18] Intentionally ignoring the formless, chaotic *something* over which, according to Genesis 1:2, God "hovered" or "moved" as God shaped, crafted, and summoned life, those early theologians asserted instead a God who created something out of absolutely nothing. For them, an optimally heroic deity was useful in making the case for the Christian God's superiority over His early rivals. Today, the notion of creation *ex nihilo* continues to be theologically meaningful to many. I mention it here not to engage that particular argument but because we run into a similar fascination with the heroic when it comes to understandings of the work of Christ.

This fascination tends to obscure the fact that Jesus spent a whole lot of time doing nonheroic work: walking beside those who were heavy-laden; caring for the sick, the infirmed, the outcast, and the prisoner; telling stories rooted in everyday experiences; sharing simple meals with friends and strangers. Given this, perhaps what is truly extraordinary is that people looked at this average, ordinary man and saw *God.* The extraordinary message of the incarnation may well be that God is to be encountered *in* the ordinary—in flesh, blood, and finitude; in the bread that is broken for all and the cup that is shared with everyone; in the everyday, nonheroic ways we carry out our lives and complete our work. A miraculous birth, the performance of

> Jesus spent a whole lot of time doing nonheroic work: walking beside those who were heavy-laden; caring for the sick, the infirmed, the outcast, and the prisoner; telling stories rooted in everyday experiences; sharing simple meals with friends and strangers.

miracles, rising from the dead—from one perspective, these are obfuscations. The heroisms get in the way of our seeing that God is here, now, in the mundane work of everyday life. Maybe the task of faithful living begins with the removal of our star-gazing glasses and a return to plain vision.

Dwelling on Jesus' nonheroic yet still life-giving work may help us see and appreciate the vital importance of the nonheroic workers all around us: the ones on whose backs the nations have been built and without whose labor the wheels of industry and commerce would come to a screeching halt. How easy it is to forget that whatever we are able to "create" with our work or consume with our wealth is indebted to the blood, sweat, and tears of countless others. Truly, our work is not our own. We stand on the shoulders of so many, depending on the foundations others have laid, the sacrifices others have made. We receive their work as a gift, not of our making, wholly undeserved.

What if, instead of ignoring or denying our rootedness in the so-called nothing-work of the masses, those in the professional and management classes *hovered over* this abyss, this deep, deep pool of labor that traditional economics devalues and dehumanizes? Instead of vanquishing or mastering it, what if we declared common cause, connecting our work to the work of the masses? Most Americans like to think of ourselves as a classless society, but we might "hover" over the possibility that this is an illusion that only serves to deepen the divides. When we do think in terms of class, the vast majority of us identify up—that is, we associate ourselves with a higher class than the one to which we actually belong. Such aspirational thinking seems harmless enough, except that it motivates us to identify our own well-being with those above us and to make decisions that are at cross-purposes with our own good and with the common good. The tendency in our society is to conflate class with income or culture (fashion, taste), but as we have seen in this book, a better indicator of class in our day might be the degree of freedom we have to determine the shape and outcomes of our work.[19] Considered in this light, more than 60 percent of us are working class, more than 30 percent are middle class, and only 2 percent are upper class.[20] Middle-class Christians may feel profoundly uncomfortable with this kind of talk about class—after all, we are invested both emotionally and financially, through 401(k) plans and the like, in the success of the upper class. We do, indeed, identify up. Nevertheless, there can be little doubt that the weight of our religious tradition calls us to identify *down*—to see and appreciate the nonheroic work all around us and, through our own work, to help share the goods of creation with all.

Meditating on the implications of Jesus the Christ for our daily work might also bring to mind the central claim of Christianity that God became human. In the person of Jesus of Nazareth, God's saving intention for the world is literally bodied forth, made concrete and tangible. In the incarnation, God embraces material existence. God loves the world so much that God becomes part of it. For Christians, the incarnation means Platonic dualism is not an option. The material realm may bear the limitations of finitude, but it is shot through with divine presence and vitality. Bodies, flesh, earth—these things matter to God; they are beloved by God. When it comes to work, the incarnation calls the lie on the propensity to denigrate manual labor in favor of intellectual work. In the midst of all the conveniences and opportunities of computer technologies and digital advances, and even while celebrating the contributions of intellectual and spiritual work, Christians will want to keep an eye on the body and the earth. As an incarnation people, we will be especially attuned to the human and environmental impact of new technologies and methodologies. Along with the pulp and paper factory workers we encountered in chapter 1, we will want to consider the losses incurred by the computerization of work—the disappearance of work's rich sentience and of tangible, embodied connections to one's labor.

Christian tradition offers rich resources for evaluating work in today's complex and fast-moving world and for pushing back against practices and structures that are at odds with an economy of grace. Like everyone else today, Christians find themselves neck-deep in both the advances and benefits of capitalist economy *and* its disfigurements of self, community, and creation. In this book, we have been groping our way toward a Christian re-formation of work that makes the blessings of creation—including work as survival, selfhood, and service—available to all. We have recognized that religion and church are perhaps uniquely poised, and therefore called, to provide a robust counternarrative to traditional economy's tendency to reduce work to just another commodity of exchange and competition. In an economy of grace, we have suggested, work is plentiful and participatory. It is God's gift to us and our gift to others. In God's economy, there are no owners, only fellow workers with the common aim of life abundant for all. Now, let's get to work.

notes

Introduction
1. Zygmunt Bauman, "Life on Credit," *Soundings* 41, no. 1 (2009): 56–64.

Chapter 1. Working: Beyond Survival
1. The discussion in this paragraph is based on the work of William Julius Wilson. See, for example, "Jobless Poverty: A New Form of Social Dislocation in the Inner-City Ghetto," in *Working in America: Continuity, Conflict, and Change*, 3rd ed., ed. Amy S. Wharton (Boston: McGraw-Hill, 2006), 178.

2. Ibid., 180.

3. *Universal Declaration of Human Rights*, Adopted and proclaimed by General Assembly resolution 217 A (III) of 10 December 1948. Available at http://www.wunrn.com/reference/pdf/univ_dec_hum_right.pdf (accessed February 6, 2011).

4. Information on homeless recyclers comes from Teresa Gowan, "American Untouchables: Homeless Scavengers in San Francisco's Underground Economy," in Wharton, *Working in America*, 447–58.

5. Ibid., 454.

6. Ibid., 452.

7. Ibid., 458.

8. Paula M. Rayman, *Beyond the Bottom Line: The Search for Dignity at Work* (New York: Palgrave, 2001), 94.

9. Lars Svendsen, *Work* (Stocksfield: Acumen, 2008), 38.

10. "Consumption," *Merriam-Webster Online Dictionary* (2011 Merriam-Webster, Incorporated). Available at http://www.merriam-webster.com/dictionary/consumption (accessed February 6, 2011).

11. Frederick Taylor, *The Principles of Scientific Management* (1911). Available at http://nationalhumanitiescenter.org/pds/gilded/progress/text3/taylor.pdf.

12. Stephen Meyer III, "The Evolution of the New Industrial Technology," in Wharton, *Working in America*, 43.

13. Ibid.

14. For a description of the 24/7 temporality of contemporary work, see my essay, "It's About Time: Reflections on a Theology of Rest" in *Theology That Matters: Ecology, Economy, and God*, edited by Darby Kathleen Ray (Minneapolis: Fortress Press, 2006), 154–71.

15. Sociologists Steven Vallas and John Beck offer a helpful summary of post-Fordist theory in their essay "The Transformation of Work Revisited: The Limits of Flexibility in American Manufacturing," in Wharton, *Working in America*, 136–54.

16. Cited in Shoshana Zuboff, "In the Age of the Smart Machine," in Wharton, *Working in America*, 116.

17. Vallas and Beck, "The Transformation of Work Revisited," 147.

18. Mike Rose, *The Mind at Work: Valuing the Intelligence of the American Worker* (New York: Penguin, 2004), xviii.

19. Edna Bonacich and Richard P. Appelbaum, "Behind the Label: The Return of the Sweatshop," in Wharton, *Working in America*, 289.

20. Ibid., 292.

21. Information in this paragraph is based on "Are We Not Temps?" by Jackie Krasas Rogers, in Wharton, *Working in America*, 435–45.

22. The discussion of Experience Unlimited is based on Vicki Smith, "Structural Unemployment and the Reconstruction of the Self in the Turbulent Economy," in Wharton, *Working in America*, 94–112.

23. Cited in Vicki Smith, "Structural Unemployment and the Reconstruction of the Self," in Wharton, *Working in America*, 108.

24. See James A. Evans, Gideon Kunda, and Stephen R. Barley, "Beach Time, Bridge Time, and Billable Hours: The Temporal Structure of Technical Contracting," in Wharton, *Working in America*, 564–89.

25. Arlie Russell Hochschild, "The Managed Heart," in Wharton, *Working in America*, 69–78.

26. Ibid., 71.

27. Ibid.

28. Arlie Russell Hochschild, "Love and Gold," in Wharton, *Working in America*, 492.

29. Ibid., 493.

30. Ibid., 490.

Chapter 2. Biblical Insights into Working

1. Hesiod's eighth-century B.C.E. admonition to his audience that "in work there is no shame" because "the gods have given work to men" is often included in discussions and anthologies of work as the exception that proves the rule of Greek negativity when it comes to work. Hesiod, "Works and Days," in *Hesiod and Theognis*, trans. Dorothea Wender (Baltimore: Penguin, 1973), 68–71.

2. Plato, *The Republic* (Chicago: Regnery, 1942), book 2.

3. Ibid.

4. Aristotle, *The Politics* (VII, iii) as presented in *Working: Its Meaning and Its Limits*, ed. Gilbert C. Meilaender (Notre Dame, Ind.: University of Notre Dame Press, 2000), 59.

5. The quotations in this paragraph are from Aristotle, *Nicomachean Ethics*, in Meilaender, *Working: Its Meaning and Its Limits*, 56–59.

6. M. Douglas Meeks, *God the Economist: The Doctrine of God and Political Economy* (Minneapolis: Fortress Press, 1989).

Chapter 3. Insights from Christian Tradition

1. Among the many examples are two that have especially informed this chapter: Lars Svendsen, *Work* (Stocksfield: Acumen, 2008), ch. 1; and Lee Hardy, *The Fabric of This World: Inquiries into Calling, Career Choice, and the Design of Human Work* (Grand Rapids: Eerdmans, 1990), chs. 1–2.

2. Pope Innocent III, *On the Misery of the Human Condition*. Cited in Gloria Fiero, *The Humanistic Tradition*, book 2, *Medieval Europe and the World Beyond* (Boston: McGraw-Hill, 2002), 97.

3. John of Salisbury, *Statesman's Handbook*, cited in Robert Sessions and Jack Wortman, eds., *Working in America: A Humanities Reader* (Notre Dame, Ind.: University of Notre Dame Press, 1992), 186.

4. Martin Luther, "Freedom of a Christian," in *Martin Luther: Selections from His Writings*, ed. John Dillenberger (New York: Anchor, 1961), 62.

5. Ibid., 64.

6. Quoted by Hardy, *The Fabric of This World*, 59.

7. Luther, "Freedom of a Christian," 67.

8. The quotations in this paragraph are from John Calvin, *Institutes of the Christian Religion*, cited in Gilbert C. Meilaender, ed., *Working: Its Meaning and Its Limits* (Notre Dame, Ind.: University of Notre Dame Press, 2000), 107.

9. Ibid.

10. Ibid.

11. Ibid., 61.

12. See, for example, "A Treatise of the Vocations or Callings of Men," in *The Work of William Perkins*, ed. Ian Breward (Appleford, United Kingdom: Sutton Courtenay, 1970), 250–69.

13. Quoted in Gary Dorrien, *Economy, Difference, Empire: Social Ethics for Social Justice* (New York: Columbia University Press, 2010), 12. Dorrien's book is a key source throughout this section of the book.

14. For further discussion of Gladden and the Social Gospel, see Bradley W. Bateman, "The Social Gospel and the Progressive Era," *Divining America: Religion in American History*, Teacher Serve, National Humanities Center, http://nationalhumanitiescenter .org/tserve/twenty/tkeyinfo/socgospel.htm (accessed November 15, 2010).

15. "Washington Gladden," *GIGA Quotes*, http://www.giga-usa .com/quotes/authors/washington_gladden_a001.htm (accessed December 15, 2010).

16. Quoted in Dorrien, *Economy, Difference, Empire*, 8.

17. Ibid., 17.

18. Walter Rauschenbusch, *Christianity and the Social Crisis* (New York: Macmillan, 1907), 235.

19. Ibid., 234.

20. Ibid., 234–35.

21. Ibid., 244, 265.

22. Ibid., 244.

23. Ibid., 246.

24. Ibid., 252.

25. For a full treatment of this claim, see Dorrien, *Economy, Difference, Empire*.

26. Ibid., 20.

27. Ibid., 19.

28. Ibid., 23.

29. Information presented in this paragraph and the next is based on a 2001 essay written by Jay P. Dolan, Professor of History at the University of Notre Dame, for a conference hosted on the twentieth anniversary of *Laborem Exercens* by the Pontifical Council for Justice and Peace on the theme of "Work as Key to the Social Question: The Great Social and Economic Transformations and the Subjective Dimension of Work." Dolan's paper, "From Charity to Justice: The Emergence of a Catholic Social Gospel," is available at *Laborem Exercens Conference,* Center for Catholic Studies, John A. Ryan Institute, University of St. Thomas, http://www.stthomas.

edu/cathstudies/CST/conferences/LE/papers/Dolan.pdf(accessed December 1, 2010).

30. Pope John Paul II, *Laborem Exercens* (1981), available online at *Catholic Social Teaching,* Office for Social Justice, St. Paul, Minn., http://www.osjspm.org/majordoc_laborem_exercens_official_text.aspx (accessed December 1, 2010).

31. Ibid.

32. Ibid.

33. The quotations in this paragraph are from ibid.

34. Ibid.

Chapter 4. Toward a Sacramental Theology of Work

1. For a compelling theological exploration of this theme in light of contemporary economic and ecological challenges, see Sallie McFague, *Life Abundant: Rethinking Theology and Economy for a Planet in Peril* (Minneapolis: Fortress Press, 2001).

2. For an insightful and moving interpretation of work and Eucharist, as well as of work as gift, see David H. Jensen, *Responsive Labor: A Theology of Work* (Louisville: Westminster John Knox, 2006).

3. Kathryn Tanner, *Economy of Grace* (Minneapolis: Fortress Press, 2005), 26–27.

4. Adam Smith, *Wealth of Nations* (London: T. Nelson and Sons, 1864), 28.

5. One company that was inspired by Judeo-Christian values to make this change is Precision Manufacturing in Minneapolis, where management changed its practices to achieve a living wage for all employees while still maintaining product excellence and financial viability. See Michael J. Naughton, "Distributors of Justice: A Case for a Just Wage" in *America* (New York: America Press, Inc., June 2000), 165–67.

6. See http://www.livingwage.geog.psu.edu/.

7. Barbara Ehrenreich, *Nickel and Dimed: On (Not) Getting By in America* (New York: Metropolitan, 2001), 106.

8. William Greider, *The Soul of Capitalism: Opening Paths to a Moral Economy* (New York: Simon & Schuster, 2003), 17.

9. The discussion of Mondragón is largely based on the article by David Herrera, "Mondragón: A For-Profit Organization That Embodies Catholic Social Thought" (paper presented at 5th International Symposium on Catholic Social Thought and Management Education, Bilbao, Spain, July 15–18, 2003), available at *Bilbao Conference: Schedule and Papers Presented*, Center for Catholic Studies, John A. Ryan Institute, University of St. Thomas,

www.stthomas.edu/cathstudies/cst/conferences/bilbao/papers/ Herrera.pdf (accessed December 1, 2010).

10. While many sources cite the start-up failure rate as 70–90 percent, U.S. Department of Commerce data show that about half of new firms last for five years or more. See "What is the survival rate for new firms?" at http://www.sba.gov/advocacy/7495/8430 (accessed February 5, 2011).

11. Barbara Brown Taylor, "The Work of Being Human," in *The Meaning of Work: A Resource for the Theological Exploration of Vocation at Hastings College* (Hastings, Neb.: Hastings College, 2004), 2:11–14.

12. For a full discussion of this point, see my book *Incarnation and Imagination: A Christian Ethic of Ingenuity* (Minneapolis: Fortress Press, 2008), ch. 3, "Making a Way out of No Way: Christic Imagination in African American Tradition."

13. Benjamin E. Mays and Joseph W. Nicholson, "The Genius of the Negro Church," in *Afro-American Religious History: A Documentary Witness*, ed. Milton Sernett (Durham: Duke University Press, 1985), 340.

14. For a fuller consideration of Sabbath in relation to work in today's 24/7 economy, see my essay "It's about Time: Reflections on a Theology of Rest," in *Theology That Matters: Ecology, Economy, and God*, ed. Darby Kathleen Ray (Minneapolis: Fortress Press, 2006), 154–71.

15. For classic insights into Sabbath, see Abraham Joshua Heschel, *The Sabbath: Its Meaning for Modern Man* (New York: Farrar, Straus & Giroux, 1951), 10.

16. Wayne Muller, *Sabbath: Finding Rest, Renewal, and Delight in Our Busy Lives* (New York: Bantam, 1999), 6.

17. For a more developed consideration of the work of Christ, see my *Deceiving the Devil: Atonement, Ransom, and Abuse* (Cleveland: Pilgrim, 1998).

18. See Catherine Keller, *Face of the Deep: A Theology of Becoming* (London: Routledge, 2002).

19. For a compelling discussion of class, see Joerg Rieger, *No Rising Tide: Theology, Economics, and the Future* (Minneapolis: Fortress Press, 2009).

20. Rieger cites Michael Zweig, *The Working Class Majority: America's Best Kept Secret* (Ithaca, N.Y.: Cornell University Press, 2001), 10, 34–35.

suggestions for further reading

Dorrien, Gary. *Economy, Difference, Empire: Social Ethics for Social Justice*. New York: Columbia University Press, 2010.

Ehrenreich, Barbara. *Nickel and Dimed: On (Not) Getting by in America*. New York: Metropolitan Books, 2001.

Hardy, Lee. *The Fabric of this World: Inquiries into Calling, Career, Choice, and the Design of Human Work*. Grand Rapids: Eerdmans, 1990.

Jensen, David H. *Responsive Labor: A Theology of Work*. Louisville: Westminster John Knox, 2006.

McFague, Sallie. *Life Abundant: Rethinking Theology and Economy for a Planet in Peril*. Minneapolis: Fortress Press, 2001.

Meeks, M. Douglas. *God the Economist: The Doctrine of God and Political Economy*. Minneapolis: Fortress Press, 1989.

Meilaender, Gilbert C. *Working: Its Meaning and Its Limits*. Notre Dame, Ind.: University of Notre Dame Press, 2000.

Muller, Wayne. *Sabbath: Finding Rest, Renewal, and Delight in Our Busy Lives*. New York: Bantam, 1999.

Rayman, Paula, M. *Beyond the Bottom Line: The Search for Dignity at Work*. New York: Palgrave, 2001.

Rieger, Joerg. *No Rising Tide: Theology, Economics, and the Future*. Minneapolis: Fortress Press, 2009.

Rose, Mike. *The Mind at Work: Valuing the Intelligence of the American Worker*. New York: Penguin, 2004.

Svendsen, Lars. *Work*. Stocksfield, United Kingdom: Acumen, 2008.

Tanner, Kathryn. *Economy of Grace*. Minneapolis: Fortress Press, 2005.

Wharton, Amy S. *Working in America: Continuity, Conflict, and Change*. Boston: McGraw-Hill, 2006.

reader's guide

Consider your own world of work. What about your work brings you joy or fulfillment? What depletes or diminishes you? Have you ever been involuntarily unemployed? If so, what challenges did that pose to your physical, emotional, and/or spiritual well-being?

Of the specific worlds of work described in chapter 1, choose one that speaks to you. What is it about that world that interests, moves, or challenges you?

Consider the biblical passages on work highlighted in chapter 2. Which ones speak to your experience? Are there passages that you find especially comforting or *dis*comforting? Given the range of biblical perspectives on work, are there points of consensus or frequent emphasis that might allow you to make some generalizations about a "biblical" view of work?

What insights into work from Christian tradition (chapter 3) do you find compelling?

Are Reformation notions of work as calling and/or service relevant to today's world? What are the dangers or consequences of overvaluing work?

Over a century ago, the Social Gospel movement considered Christian scripture and doctrine in the light of the harsh realities of working-class existence and concluded that the church has a moral obligation to press for a more just and humane organization of work. Catholic social teachings arrived at the same conclusion. Most people would agree that conditions are better for workers today than they were in the late nineteenth century, but have we come far enough in making work a humanizing experience? Are there specific insights from the Social Gospel and/or Catholic social teachings that are especially germane to today's situation?

What difference might it make if we were to consider work as one of the gifts of creation, freely given by God for the benefit of all? What might the implications be for your own workplace? Your church?

How could your work and life benefit from habits of deep rest? Reflect on some specific Sabbath practices you could implement in your own life. Resolve to take the first step toward implementing one such practice.

On what kinds of nonheroic work does your daily life depend?

What difference might it make if you were to think of your own work as both God's gift to you and your gift to others?